Battles

David Owen

Battles

50 of history's most important conflicts

NH
NEW
HOLLAND

Contents

6   Introduction

8   Part One: Ancient and Medieval Warfare
Shock Action - Arbela 331 BCE • Ambush at Cannae - Cannae
216 BCE • Double-sided Siege - Alesia 52 BCE • Forest Ambush
- Teutoburg Forest 9 CE • Rash Attack - Hastings 1066 •
Terror Tactics - Bokhara 1220 • Clever Use of Ground -
Bannockburn 1314 • Triumph of the Longbow - Crécy 1346

28   Part Two: Nation in Arms
Reforming Army - Breitenfeld 1631 • Victory of Discipline -
Naseby 1645 • Tactics of Deception - Blenheim 1704 • Prussian
Speed and Discipline - Leuthen 1757 • Riflemen Overcome
Regular Army - Cowpens 1781 • Advent of Mass Warfare - Valmy
1792 • Speed and Mobility - Austerlitz 1805 • Defence in
Depth - Torres Vedras 1811 • Frontal Attacks Prove Costly -
Borodino 1812 • A Linear Defence - Waterloo 1815 • Napoleonic
Tactics in America - Chancellorsville 1863 • Fortified
Positions - Gettysburg 1863

58   Part Three: Wars of Empire
Numerical Advantage Overturned - Plassey 1757 • A Siege
Against the Odds - Delhi 1857 • Courage and Mobility -
Isandlwana 1879 • Defence Against Mass Attacks - Rorke's
Drift 1879

70   Part Four: World Wars
Speed Defeats Two Armies - Tannenburg 1914• Failed Landings
Prepare for D-Day - Gallipoli 1915 • Strategy of Attrition -
Verdun and the Somme 1916 • Ending Stalemate - Amiens 1918 •

Blitzkrieg Breakthrough - France 1940 • Cutting off a
Retreat - North Africa 1941 • Japanese Back-door
Invasion - Singapore 1942 • A Return to Trench Warfare -
El Alamein 1942 • Defeating Blitzkrieg - Russia 1943 •
Countering Mobile Forces - Stalingrad 1943 • Honing Air
Bombardment - Tarawa 1943 • Success of a Seaborne
Invasion - Normandy 1944

102 Part Five: Modern Wars
The Fortress that Failed - Dien Bien Phu 1954 •
The Media in Warfare - Tet Offensive 1968 • Shock
and Firepower - Desert Storm 1991

110 Part Six: Naval War
New Naval Tactics - Spanish Armada 1588 • Royal Navy's
Deadly Fire - Trafalgar 1805 • A Key Role for Battleships
- Tsushima 1905 • Pre-emptive Strikes - Pearl Harbor 1941
• Ships of the Future - Midway 1942 • U-boat Stranglehold
- Battle of the Atlantic 1943 • Long-distance Landing -
Falklands War 1982

128 Part Seven: Aerial Battles
First Long-range Aerial Bombing - England 1915 • Radar's
Key Role - Battle of Britain 1940 • Hamburg Firestorm -
Battle of Hamburg 1943 • Kamikaze Attacks - North
Pacific 1944-45

140   Glossary
141   Sources
142   Index

Introduction

From before the dawn of recorded history, warfare has been one of the most powerful forces shaping the development of humankind. Only if a community had the strength, the intelligence and the motivation to defeat outside attackers trying to steal its possessions and enslave its people, would it thrive and prosper. As local settlements grew into towns and cities and eventually entire nations, these struggles became more complex and more essential for survival. Ultimately natural resources, prosperity and culture counted for little without the means for self-defence: the strategies, tactics and weapons to defeat those of their enemies.

This book shows how this essential art of warfare became more sophisticated with the passing of the centuries. Through examining the ideas and tactics used in 50 key battles ranging in time from Alexander the Great in battle against the Persian Empire 2,300 years ago to Desert Storm in 1991, it explains how each new idea managed to overturn the existing balance of power until a new counter-development brought another change in its turn, and so on. New weapons, for example, can help overturn the dominance of a nation and the way it fights its battles. From the mailed horseman to the longbow, from cannon balls to explosive shells, each advance in weaponry can prove decisive in each new confrontation. Yet through the long and violent history of warfare, each new weapon also has a finite shelf-life. Eventually it will meet its counter, as the tank produced the anti-tank gun, and the submarine the depth charge.

The course and significance of each battle is outlined, including explanations of the effects of new weapons, new theatres of operations, new tactics and new objectives on the story. Each entry covers the background, the state of the military art at the time, the strengths and weaknesses of the adversaries, the immediate outcome of the battle and its significance in the wider history of warfare.

The story begins with the ancient and medieval worlds, where armoured horsemen and foot soldiers fought with sword and shield, lance and battleaxe, crossbow and longbow, to win their battles. Tactics remained simple, but often could produce remarkable results, with long-lasting effects on battles centuries later. Radical developments soon followed, with much more powerful weapons like rifles and muskets, guns and howitzers. Social and political changes saw armies increase in size and expertise from groups of slaves or volunteers to trained and professional armies and eventually entire nations in arms as conflicts grew in scale. Wars ranged from struggles between nation states and their allies to the establishment of empires on a global scale.

The process reaches its peak with the two great world wars of the 20th century, which saw such huge advances in training, in command, in communications, in intelligence, in firepower, in tactics, in every facet of military operations in theatres ranging from empty deserts to remote mountain ranges and from the deepest jungles to crowded cities.

Finally, the story turns to more recent battles, set against remote and exotic backgrounds ranging from Vietnam and the Falklands to Iraq. It covers air and naval battles for dramatic examples of how world events are determined by clashes between ships and aircraft instead of cavalry and artillery, armour and infantry. Yet throughout this long and vivid history of conflict, some themes have remained enduring and unchanging. So long as war exists, the story of battles offers a fascinating insight into the importance of ideas and motivation, courage and sacrifice, as forces shaping human destiny. And whatever else may change on the battlefields of the future, these virtues will remain as a counterpoint to the cruelty and casualties of warfare.

Part One:
Ancient and Medieval Warfare

Shock Action

Where:	Arbela, near Nineveh – now northern Iraq
When:	331 BCE
War:	Alexander's campaign of conquest (336–323 BCE)
Combatants:	Macedonia vs. Persian Empire
Casualties:	Macedonians: 2,000–4,000; Persians: 40,000–90,000

By 331 BCE, Alexander of Macedonia – the legendary Alexander the Great – had conquered Syria and Egypt, but the Persian emperor, Darius the Great, was assembling a huge army to crush him, with infantry and cavalry reinforced by archers and war chariots. Leaving nothing to chance, Darius chose the level plain of Arbela, near the ruins of Nineveh in northern Iraq, to face Alexander's onslaught. Here, his huge army could deploy and manoeuvre easily.

The Positions

Alexander's 47,000 troops were heavily outnumbered by between 50,000 and 100,000 Persians. Darius followed convention in placing his infantry in the centre, with cavalry on both wings. He arranged his chariots in front of his army, ready to charge while his archers would fire volleys of arrows against the invaders. He waited for Alexander's forces to make the first move.

Like Darius, Alexander massed his phalanx of heavy infantry in the centre, with cavalry on both wings. Having smaller numbers, he occupied a narrower front, which allowed him to place a fast-moving reserve force of cavalry and light infantry behind each wing. Should the wider mass of the Persian army try to envelop his smaller formation, these reserves could rush to reinforce any weak points in his lines. His masterstroke, however, was to shift the entire balance of his forces so that his right wing was much stronger, and would be able to deliver the decisive blow.

The Battle

Alexander sent his phalanx advancing towards the Persians but with each wing arranged in a reversed diagonal formation – an exposure calculated to provoke a Persian cavalry attack. When they charged, the Persians left open vulnerable gaps in the centre of Darius's army – gaps, which in Alexander's army, the fast-moving light infantry closed. The long and deadly spears carried by the Macedonians soon neutralized Darius's chariots – they channelled each into one of several gaps in their front rank, so that horse and rider could be trapped and killed by those in the ranks behind.

While the Persians spread out across the field and began driving back the Macedonian left flank, Alexander gathered together his reserves into a massive wedge-shaped formation and launched a huge blow at the gap in the centre of the Persian ranks, tearing through the defenders and forcing them back on both sides of the wedge. By this time, his deliberately weakened left flank was crumbling under Persian attack, offering Darius a brief hope of victory, but it was already too late. The Persians had to flee Alexander's attack, knowing their cause was lost. Eventually Alexander could turn and rescue his battered left wing, having won the battle.

The Outcome and Significance

Darius escaped, together with Bessius, the commander of the left wing of his army. Bessius murdered him before he could raise another army, only to be slain himself a year later by the pursuing Alexander. The Macedonians were now effectively masters of the Persian Empire, with even greater conquests in prospect.

Alexander's inspiration had been to use shock action to defeat an enemy that was scenting victory right up to the moment that he delivered his decisive blow. Even using foot soldiers and simple weapons, the battle demonstrated just how effective shock action could be. His tactics provided an enduring model for commanders across the centuries, who used them to great effect – first with cavalry and, later, using armoured formations.

Ambush at Cannae

Where: Cannae, Eastern Italy
When: 216 BCE
War: Second Punic War (218–210 BCE)
Combatants: Carthagian Empire vs.
              Roman Empire
Casualties: Carthaginians: 6,000;
              Romans: 70,000

For almost 50 years, the Roman Empire had been battling against the North African empire of Carthage for Mediterranean supremacy. In the autumn of 218 BCE, Carthaginian commander, Hannibal, led an army from Spain across the Alps, to attack his enemy in its homeland. Though almost half his men died on the journey, he won battle after battle in Italy but as he failed to win allies against Roman rule, what he needed most was a decisive victory.

The Positions

By the summer of 216 BCE, the Romans had massed a force of 85,000 trained legionaries against Hannibal's army of barely half this size. But Hannibal chose the battleground, on the plain of Cannae in Umbria, and tempted his opponents to deliver an overwhelming attack on his smaller force.

He placed his heavy infantry in the centre of his line, in a curved formation facing the enemy, and between wings of lighter infantry, which were able to move and respond quickly. This curved formation was the bait for his trap: once the Romans saw it as the focal point of his defences, they would undoubtedly launch the mass of their army to crush it. The weight of the Roman onslaught would push Hannibal's infantry back. This was his gamble. To drive deeper into the centre of his position, the Romans must reinforce the attack. Eventually, they would push the Carthaginian defenders back into a concave arc. If Hannibal's men held firm, the Romans would be fighting their way into a terrible trap. The two wings of Hannibal's army would simply need to swing inwards, surrounding their attackers. The Romans would be unable to manoeuvre or even defend themselves properly.

The Battle

Hannibal's gamble paid off. As the Carthaginian centre fell back, the Roman commanders sent more and more of their troops into the trap. By this time, Hannibal's heavy cavalry had forced the Roman horsemen from the battlefield, and were able to return to the fray. When he gave the order, the infantry of the two wings of his army, backed up by both light and heavy cavalry, swung in to crush their opponents.

The Outcome and Significance

Hannibal's encirclement of the Roman army enabled him to win one of the most decisive victories in military history. His tactics amounted to a massive ambush, luring his enemy into an unwise attack to trap and annihilate him. When the battle was over, the enemy's dead outnumbered his entire army.

Hannibal's victory did not last, however; he continued to fight new Roman armies for the next 13 years, until finally defeated and forced into exile. His nation was enslaved, as Rome henceforth refused to compromise with enemies, a philosophy that brought the Romans the greatest empire of its time.

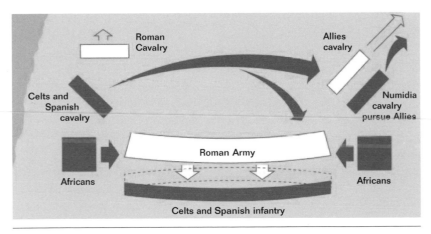

Above Hannibal's infantry was drawn up in a curved formation (dotted line); when his troops were driven back into a concave arc, the wings of his army encircled his enemy and the returning cavalry closed the trap.

Double-sided Siege

Where:	Alesia, Gaul – now southern France
When:	52 BCE
War:	Gallic Wars (58–51 BCE)
Combatants:	Roman Empire vs. Gaul
Casualties:	Romans: 12,000;
	Gauls: 40,000

Under the Roman Empire, soldiers were professionals on lifetime service under ferocious discipline. Training was continuous, and equipment carefully chosen to suit legionary tactics. Skilled engineers supported the fighting troops, laying out a sophisticated road system across the empire, and were capable of the most amazing achievements on campaign. In the late summer of 52 BCE, Julius Caesar's Roman army was fighting rebellious Gallic tribes led by their chieftain, Vercingetorix. The Gauls had decided to winter in Alesia, a formidable fortress in the mountains of eastern France. Since frontal attack was impossible, Caesar settled for a prolonged siege.

The Positions

The Romans spent three weeks building an 18-kilometre (11-mile) long wall, 4 metres (13 feet) high, right around the fortress, protected by dry and flooded ditches and studded with towers carrying siege catapults sited to bombard the 80,000 soldiers and civilians trapped inside. In places, natural obstacles caused gaps in the ramparts and the Gauls made determined cavalry attacks to disrupt construction. Finally, one group managed to force through one of the gaps and escape.

Expecting a relieving Gallic force to arrive to raise the siege, Caesar ordered his troops to build a second, even larger set of fortifications. These stretched more than 20 kilometres (12 miles) outside the existing works, but faced outwards this time, and enclosed a large enough area to protect all of Caesar's troops.

The Battle

The relieving army of some 100,000 Gauls appeared in the last week of September. Normally this would have been enough to drive off Caesar's 60,000 men, especially if the 80,000 Gauls within the fortress joined in. Yet, when they attacked the Roman fortifications on 30 September, fighting lasted from midday to dusk without the legions giving way. They attacked again the following evening but only drove the Romans back from some of their positions. Finally, they launched a last desperate effort on 2 October, with 60,000 men attacking one of the weak points in the outer wall, and another 60,000 from within the fortress attacking the inner wall.

This time numbers began to tell. Caesar rode up and down cheering his troops on to buttress morale. He sent the commander of his German cavalry, Labienus, to drive off the attackers from the outer wall, while he led counterattacks to defend the inner wall. These were successful at the precise moment that it became clear the defence of the outer walls was about to break.

Desperate measures were needed. Caesar took some 6,000 cavalry from his own force and rode outside the fortifications to charge the Gauls outside the wall, turning the tables completely. The Romans cheered to see their commander risking everything to come to their relief, while the Gauls found themselves surrounded and morale collapsed. They turned and ran, and Caesar's cavalry set off in hot pursuit, wreaking terrible slaughter. Within hours, the battle was over, and the surviving Gauls retreated back into their fortress.

The Outcome and Significance

Vercingetorix, seeing all hope of relief vanishing over the horizon, capitulated the following day and was taken as a prisoner to Rome for execution. Every legionary was given a Gallic slave, and Caesar himself returned to Rome in triumph. Julius Caesar had turned a complex siege operation into a double-sided envelopment that enabled him to defeat a large relieving army as well as those inside the fortress he was attacking. Over the years, siege craft became more complex with stone fortifications and gunpowder weapons but Caesar's victory at Alesia, for a loss of 12,000 soldiers, would never be surpassed.

Forest Ambush

Where:	Teutoburg Forest, Germany
When:	9 CE
War:	Roman campaign against the Germanic tribes (12 BCE–17 CE)
Combatants:	Roman Empire vs. Germanic tribes
Casualties:	Romans: 20,000–25,000; Germanic tribes: not known, but almost certainly fewer

Rigorous training, careful tactics and proven fighting methods had turned the Roman legions into the most formidable military machine. However, all fighting forces remain potentially vulnerable to new tactics and fighting methods. In the year 9 CE, the Germanic chieftain, Arminius, a trusted Roman ally, forged a secret alliance between six different tribes to rebel against the Roman advance into his homeland.

The Positions

Three legions, the 17th, 18th and 19th, were sent on a punitive expedition into German territory with Arminius as a guide. With three squadrons of cavalry and accompanied by auxiliaries and camp followers, the force was unable to march along the narrow tracks in combat formation and it straggled over 16 kilometres (10 miles). It seems likely that Arminius had deliberately chosen the route to increase the column's vulnerability. He had lived in Rome in his youth and been given military training, so he had first-hand knowledge of tactics, methods and weapons. No reconnaissance parties had been sent on ahead – probably at his advice – and he was later allowed to leave the column to summon extra support.

The Battle

German tribesmen struck on 9 September, in thick forests on the northern slopes of the Wiehen Hills in the north German province of Lower Saxony. Large groups attacked at different points along the straggling column, so the legionaries could not deploy into formation to resist. Roman training soon enabled some to establish a night camp and retreat within its ramparts for safety. The following morning, despite heavy losses, they fought their way out into open countryside, but remained surrounded by endless forests, in which their enemies waited.

They decided to retrace their steps and return to base. Endless rain had softened the archers' bowstrings and the legionaries' shields were soaked and weakened. However, Arminius had prepared a careful ambush at a point where the route narrowed into a defile between a bog and the slopes of a hill. Here the Germans dug a deep trench to block the path and built a rampart of earth and peat blocks on the forest edge, from which to attack the Romans under cover.

The result was a catastrophe for the Romans. Despite furious efforts, the legionaries failed to mount the rampart. The cavalry tried to escape the coming massacre but groups of German horsemen hunted them down and killed them. Finally, the Roman ranks thinned to allow the Germans to emerge from cover. They slaughtered most of the survivors, and took the remainder prisoner.

The Outcome and Significance

Three entire legions had been annihilated. Many officers committed suicide or were killed in the fighting and others ended as human sacrifices in the tribes' religious rites. The Germans ransomed a small number of survivors back to Rome to tell the story of their defeat. Between 15,000 and 20,000 legionaries had been killed for trifling German losses. Two other legions retreated to the Rhine, while rebels destroyed settlements to the east of the river. Later punitive expeditions used new tactics to recover all three legionary standards and to release some of the enslaved legionaries.

The battle marked the Roman Empire's first real defeat, as the clever tactics of the Germanic tribes vanquished its legions in the trackless forests. For the Romans, the defeat taught a terrible lesson – that the legions could not guarantee supremacy in all conditions and against all opponents. For the German tribes, their victory depended on local knowledge and conditions, and victories outside the forests had to wait until the empire's final decline.

Rash Attack

Where: Senlac Hill, near Hastings, England
When: 1066
War: Norman Conquest (1066)
Combatants: Saxons vs. Normans
Casualties: Saxons: 5,000; Normans: 3,000

Harold Godwinson, Earl of Wessex, and Duke William of Normandy both claimed the English throne on the death of Edward the Confessor in 1066, and William landed his army on English soil on 28 September. Three days earlier, Harold had killed another invading claimant, the Viking King Harold Hardrada, at Stamford Bridge near York. Hearing of William's arrival, he rushed his army southwards to face the invaders at Senlac Hill, 9 kilometres (6 miles) from Hastings on the morning of 14 October, 1066. While the English army of 7,500 men was composed entirely of foot soldiers, the Norman force of 8,400 contained both infantry and cavalry.

The Positions

The English army lined up on the crest of the hill, forcing the Normans to attack uphill. Harold's force included housecarls – professional soldiers loyal

Above The Bayeux Tapestry, depicting the initial Norman failure at the Battle of Hastings while attacking Harold's forces uphill.

to the king – who were formidable fighters with swords and two-handed battleaxes. Reinforcements included local nobles who led levies of less skilled and more impetuous troops. Allies and mercenaries from all over Europe reinforced William's army, drawn by promises of land and plunder. He placed his own infantry in the centre with his Breton allies on the left wing, and mainly French and Flemish troops on the right. Archers and crossbowmen were massed in front, with cavalry at the rear to exploit any breaks in the enemy line.

The Battle

William's plan was for his archers to weaken the English defenders, followed by an infantry attack to break their line and a cavalry charge for the final decisive blow. But the English deflected the arrows by locking their huge, kite-shaped shields into an armoured wall. With no English archers to fire arrows back at them, the Normans' stocks depleted quickly. Resolute and well-armed defenders beat back the Norman infantry charge in furious hand-to-hand fighting. In desperation, William launched his cavalry at the English line. With the defence still unbroken, this too failed. The Bretons fell back first, followed by the rest of the Norman army.

Harold's housecarls wisely rejected the temptation to attack but the local levies surged forward in pursuit. As they emerged into open ground, the Norman cavalry turned and charged. Most of the levies were slaughtered and only a remnant managed to fall back to line up again in front of the housecarls. The Normans regrouped and attacked again. This time, their archers fired over the shield wall into the lesser-protected rear ranks, while their infantry scattered the still badly shaken levies and drove new gaps into the shield wall. As these widened, the Norman cavalry charged again, this time with deadly results. Harold was killed and the English defence collapsed.

The Outcome and Significance

William was crowned King of England on Christmas Day, 1066. He had raised a fleet of more than 700 ships to mount the last successful invasion of England. The Battle of Hastings was also the first time infantry and cavalry had been so effectively combined on the battlefield. This established the supremacy of the armoured horseman as the most powerful weapon of the medieval army.

Terror Tactics

Where: Bokhara, present-day Uzbekistan
When: 1220
War: Mongol invasion (1209–1227)
Combatants: Mongolia vs. Persian Empire
Casualties: Not known

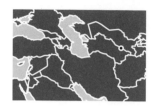

Thirteenth-century Mongol leader Genghis Khan's first conquests were in
China and within two years he had vanquished the Chinese empire, to which
Mongolia had formerly paid tribute. He then harnessed Chinese knowledge
and Chinese officers to help create an army that moved with staggering speed
to overwhelm its opponents. His soldiers used bows, scimitars and lances –
some fitted with hooks – to pull enemy horsemen from the saddle. They
carried tools, cooking utensils and rations sewn into watertight skin bags,
which could be inflated and used for crossing rivers. They and their horses
wore armour of tanned hides under overlapping metal plates – heavier for
shock attack, lighter for speed and mobility.

In 1218, Genghis Khan sent a large merchant caravan with trade
proposals to the border town of Otrar in the Persian Khwarizmian Empire
(covering the territory of modern Iran, Afghanistan, Turkestan and northern
India). The governor, Inalchuq, looted the caravan and killed the merchants.
When Mongol ambassadors to the emperor, the Shah Mohammed, were also
murdered in 1220, Genghis Khan sought a more powerful argument: his
150,000 soldiers.

The Positions

The Persians split their forces between individual fortresses but this was no
match for what was coming. Spies whispered that only instant surrender
would spare the inhabitants of cities taken by the Mongols. In fact, most were
massacred whether they fought or not. To spread fear and suspicion, Genghis
Khan used a former supporter of the Shah to write letters hinting that officers
planned to desert to the Mongols. Then followed one of the most spectacular
mobile military campaigns of all time, covering hundreds of miles in weeks.

The Mongols took Otrar first, then split into three divisions. Two carried out a pincer movement on Samarkand, while the third, led by Genghis himself, disappeared into the trackless Kizyl Kum desert, only to emerge with devastating speed and surprise to the west of the Shah's capital, Bokhara, on the river Oxus in Central Asia.

The Battle

Two walls protected the city, their outer ramparts 48 kilometres (30 miles) long, and the frightened inhabitants decided to resist. The Mongols brought up siege engines on pack animals, assembling them to batter the walls, and attacking in relays day and night to wear down resistance. Even so, breaching the outer walls proved difficult and it was months before they could attack the inner defences.

As the army prepared to attack, the defenceless citizens marched out to surrender. In fact, a number of soldiers led by the governor had retreated to the inner citadel. The Mongols, furious at being deceived by this attempt to continue resistance, set the city on fire. Most of the buildings of this great centre of Muslim learning were destroyed and the few inhabitants who survived the flames were driven out to starve in the surrounding countryside.

The Outcome and Significance

After five months' fighting, the Mongols had triumphed. The Persian Empire was destroyed and depopulated and little remained of its rich and sophisticated society. The Shah died of dysentery on an island in the Caspian Sea, while the Mongols overwhelmed Russia, Poland and Hungary and threatened Western Europe.

By combining mobility and terror, Genghis Khan had demoralized and overwhelmed his enemies time and again, his conquests ranging from China to Eastern Europe. Only their advance into the European terrain of forests and rivers hampered Mongol mobile tactics and they finally returned home. However, Khan's horsemen became a prototype for the speed and power of Napoleon's Grand Army and Hitler's panzers.

21

Clever Use of Ground

Where: Bannockburn, Scotland
When: 1314
War: Anglo–Scottish war (1296–1328)
Combatants: England vs. Scotland
Casualties: English: 12,500;
              Scots: not known, but light

In 1314 England's King Edward II, strove to regain the Scottish conquests of his father, Edward I. With a 25,000-strong army, his first priority was to raise the siege of Stirling Castle, which was of vital strategic importance, where English defenders faced a Scottish force under Edward Bruce, brother of the Scottish king. As the English approached Stirling, they met a Scottish army of just under 10,000 men, commanded by King Robert himself, an able tactician.

The core of the Scottish army consisted of four 'schiltrons' – 500-strong groups of pikemen, each fighting as a unit. At the battle of Falkirk in 1298, these had proved difficult to manoeuvre. There, Edward I's archers had broken the Scottish schiltrons led by the Guardian of Scotland, Sir William Wallace, using swarms of arrows fired from beyond the reach of their pikes. The English cavalry had then massacred the men as they fled.

The Positions

Bruce resolved not to repeat Wallace's mistakes and chose his position carefully. An open space called the Carse of Stirling was bound by streams on three sides and by the trees of a hunting reserve to the west of the main road from Falkirk. If Bruce could block the English cavalry from the road, he could divert them on to the Carse where they would lose most of their freedom of manoeuvre. To make sure, his men dug 1-metre (3-foot) deep pits, lined with spikes and covered with brushwood on both sides of the road. As the English approached, the Scottish pikemen beat off two attacks and the English fell back, as intended, on to the Carse, to camp for the night.

The Battle

During the night, the English tried to bridge the marshiest ground of the Carse so their cavalry could charge the Scottish positions. Meanwhile, Bruce drew up his four schiltrons behind a marshy brook where the ground remained too soft for cavalry, with one flank protected by a wood and the other by a bend in the stream. He also formed up 500 mounted men as a reserve force.

As the English tried to assemble on the confined space they now occupied, the Scots began to advance. Bruce sent three schiltrons forward in echelon formation, catching the English infantry off balance. As the pikes pushed them back, the English archers fired volleys of arrows but the Scottish horsemen soon rode them down, crushing them, while Bruce's bowmen lashed them with storms of arrows.

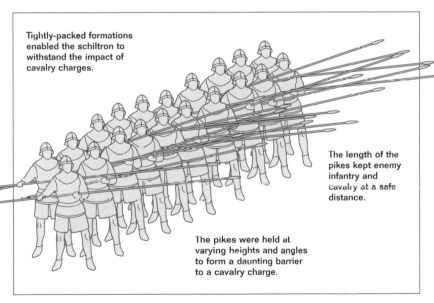

Tightly-packed formations enabled the schiltron to withstand the impact of cavalry charges.

The length of the pikes kept enemy infantry and cavalry at a safe distance.

The pikes were held at varying heights and angles to form a daunting barrier to a cavalry charge.

Above The schiltron was traditionally seen as a defensive formation, however, it was the offensive use of such formations, with their walls of spears, that proved essential in a number of battles, including Bannockburn.

At first Edward's army resisted fiercely, until Bruce's fourth schiltron emerged from hiding on their right flank to complete their encirclement. The English were now caught fast in a trap as terrible as at Cannae (see page 13). In the resulting massacre, the Scottish killed half of the English soldiers, including more than 1,000 nobles, and cut down more as they fled back to the border. Edward never returned to Scotland and it seemed the English threat was over.

The Outcome and Significance

Robert the Bruce had defeated the English army in a classic encirclement strategy – confining them to a position too small for them to deploy their forces properly. The wider lesson of Bannockburn was to demonstrate the effectiveness of a combination of massed archers and dismounted knights, the latter fighting as infantry until they were ready to remount and rout the enemy forces. This would remain a decisive strategy in warfare for more than a century.

Unfortunately, in later battles the Scots forgot that they owed their victory at Bannockburn to a clever choice of position, as well as their tactics and formations. Following the deaths of Edward II and Bruce, Edward III's army faced another Scottish host at Halidon Hill in 1333. Here, the Scots advanced rashly uphill towards a prepared English position. This time, the dismounted English knights held firm against the pikemen, while English archers cut them down with deadly fire. As they fell back, the English knights remounted and routed them, demonstrating the importance of carefully chosen positions in warfare.

Triumph of the Longbow

Where: Crécy, France
When: 1346
War: Hundred Years' War (1337–1453)
Combatants: England vs. France
Casualties: English: 90–300;
               French: 4,000–10,000

Many epic battles of the Hundred Years' War between England and France were large-scale plundering raids, seizing loot and prisoners to be ransomed for further treasure. King Edward III of England led one such expedition in 1346, when King Philip of France assembled his largest army to expel the English once and for all. Against Edward's 3,900 mounted men-at-arms and 5,000 foot soldiers, the French massed 12,000 horsemen and 20,000 foot soldiers: odds of some four to one. But the French had only 6,000 Genoese crossbowmen against 11,000 English longbowmen.

The Positions

Edward chose a secure defensive position near Abbeville in northern France, and drew his troops up in line protected by the villages of Crécy and Wadicourt, about a kilometre (¾ mile) apart. His men dismounted and split into three divisions – one led by his son, Edward the Black Prince, with his archers massed on the crest of a nearby low hill. During the long and slow French approach, the English improved their defences with ditches, barriers of wooden spikes and caltrops (sharply pointed metal obstacles) to bring down horses and deflect a cavalry charge.

The Battle

The French assumed their armoured horsemen could ride down the English archers with no difficulty. They advanced slowly behind a screen of crossbowmen, firing volleys of bolts. This proved catastrophic. Normally, crossbowmen reloaded their cumbersome weapons behind a man-high shield called a pavise but the French king insisted these be left behind. In addition, a thunderstorm had soaked their weapons, making them much less effective. Meanwhile, the English could quickly unstring their longbows, to release the tension, restringing them once conditions improved.

Edward's archers could fire up to 10 aimed shots a minute and double this rate for short periods; this was six times faster than a crossbowman.

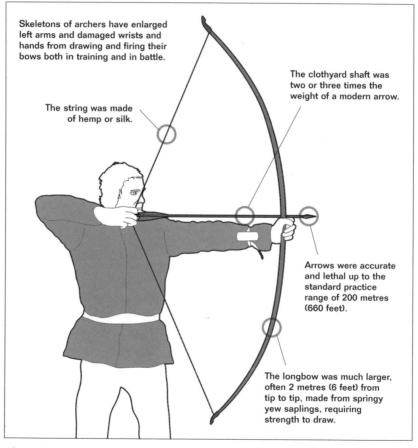

Skeletons of archers have enlarged left arms and damaged wrists and hands from drawing and firing their bows both in training and in battle.

The clothyard shaft was two or three times the weight of a modern arrow.

The string was made of hemp or silk.

Arrows were accurate and lethal up to the standard practice range of 200 metres (660 feet).

The longbow was much larger, often 2 metres (6 feet) from tip to tip, made from springy yew saplings, requiring strength to draw.

Above The effectiveness of the longbow was proven against armoured knights, contrary to the conventional tactics of the day, and ended the superiority of heavy cavalry.

When their arrows reached their targets, they could punch straight through chain mail, and even plate armour, at shorter ranges. Horses were killed or maddened with pain and became uncontrollable and the Genoese crossbowmen broke and ran, before the advancing French horsemen rode them down. However, the French knights fared no better. With hopeless courage, they charged 16 times in succession, yet a rain of arrows drove them back. As they fell, they were trapped in the increasingly muddy conditions, where English foot soldiers hacked them to pieces.

The Outcome and Significance

As the light failed, the wounded French king called a retreat. He lost between 4,000 and 10,000 men, mostly mounted knights and crossbowmen on foot, against English losses of between 90 and 300. The English kept their plunder and, at Poitiers 10 years later, the Black Prince defeated another French army by using fewer archers at the decisive moment, silencing French opposition for four more years. Finally, the lesson would be repeated in almost identical terms at Agincourt in 1415.

The tactics at Crécy emphasized the eclipse of the armoured mounted horseman as the decisive medieval weapon. The battle showed how effective archers could now be, as they were able to fire accurately from secure positions over long distances, and the longbow remained an important factor in the Hundred Years' War. Armoured cavalry would never again prove effective in warfare while, in time, archers would give way to musketeers, pikemen and artillery. Eventually, cavalry would find new roles in reconnaissance and as mounted infantry, using shock attacks only under specific conditions – a restriction that would apply to their final incarnation as the tanks of the 20th century.

Part Two:

Nation in Arms

Reforming Army

Where: Breitenfeld, near Leipzig, now
            eastern Germany
When: 1631
War: Thirty Years' War (1618–1648)
Combatants: Sweden vs. Holy Roman Empire
Casualties: Swedes: 3,000;
            Holy Roman Empire: 7,600

The Thirty Years' War involved a struggle between the Holy Roman Empire and the rising Protestant powers of Sweden, Holland, Denmark, Bohemia and their allies. In September 1631, the Imperial army advanced into Saxony in eastern Germany. By 15 September its commander, Count Tilly, had taken Leipzig but learned that the Swedes, led by King Gustavus Adolphus, were approaching. He drew up his army at Breitenfeld to meet their attack two days later.

The Positions

Tilly's 36,000 troops were massed in large squares over 12 ranks deep. Each contained up to 2,000 men, mostly pikemen, reinforced by musketeers. The Swedish army of 26,000 was split into smaller, more mobile groups, six ranks deep, each with its own cavalry and artillery with 24-pounder (11 kg) field guns and light regimental guns firing the first prepared cartridges. One horse or four men could move a light gun that could fire three shots to their opponents' one.

The Battle

The battle began with artillery. Protestant casualties were relatively light – a shot through a six-rank formation killed far fewer men than in the Imperial squares, where a shot could tear through 10 or 12 lines. Then the Imperial army attacked both Protestant flanks. The massive infantry squares, supported by light cavalry, bore down on the Saxons on Gustav's left flank, forcing the Swedes to flee, and threatening them with an encirclement.

   Meanwhile 5,000 Imperial cuirassiers – heavy cavalry with armoured breastplates – galloped around the Swedish right flank to charge from the rear and close the final gap in the encirclement. It proved fatal. The Swedes had

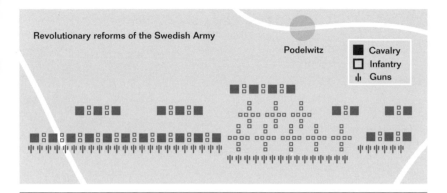

Above Instead of the traditional large squares, the Swedish Army was organized into smaller mobile units, each of which was supported by its own cavalry and artillery.

hidden a reserve line of cavalry and musketeers set further back. Instead of attacking the rear, the cuirassiers rode between the first and second Swedish lines, into a murderous crossfire, and they stood no chance at all. Finally, the Swedish cavalry fired a massive volley and routed them with a charge.

Meanwhile, Gustav swung his army to face the enemy mass on his original left flank. His opponents could not bring their heavy guns to bear, as they had sent their draft horses to the rear. In a rapid reversal of fortune, Gustav sent his right flank troops forward to seize these guns. Their fire pounded the Imperial squares to pieces, as the Swedish cavalry swung round both flanks to encircle the embattled enemy.

The Outcome and Significance

Breitenfeld was the first major Protestant victory in the war and Leipzig fell without a shot being fired. It was hailed as the first truly modern battle and inspired later commanders including Marlborough and Napoleon.

Gustav's reforms to the weapons, tactics and formations of the Swedish army had transformed it into one of the most effective fighting forces in Europe and produced a battlefield revolution. For the first time since the invention of gunpowder, movement and speed were able to defeat massive formations. Soon Gustav's revolutionary reforms would become standard tactics across Europe.

Victory of Discipline

Where: Naseby, Northamptonshire,
           England
When: 1645
War: English Civil War (1642–1651)
Combatants: Royalists vs. Parliamentarians
Casualties: Royalists: 1,000;
           Parliamentarians: 400

At the start of the English Civil War, Parliamentary cavalry proved no match for Prince Rupert's Royalist horse. Oliver Cromwell spent the war's first winter training his own horsemen into a more formidable and disciplined force and at Marston Moor in 1644, his Ironsides turned the tables at a time when Royalist victory seemed certain. By the spring of 1645, Rupert, King Charles I's nephew and deputy commander, persuaded the king to leave his Oxford headquarters and march north to gather reinforcements. Rupert took Leicester on 31 May 1645, but then had to turn back in case Oxford fell in his absence. In fact, the Roundheads had left Oxford in pursuit and, on 14 June, the two armies met at Naseby in Northamptonshire.

The Positions

The Royalist army of 9,500 occupied a strong position on a ridge at East Farndon, when Rupert spotted Parliamentary cavalry retiring ahead. He ordered his army to seize the high ground of Naseby Ridge but, with 1.6 kilometres (1 mile) to go, they saw Fairfax's 13,000-strong Roundhead army already in occupation. Rupert immediately deployed his army across 2.5 kilometres (1½ miles) between the Naseby road and a network of hedges. He placed 1,500 cavalrymen of the Northern Horse to cover the rough ground on his left, with his own horsemen on the right and the Royalist infantry in the centre.

Fairfax adopted a similar formation, with infantry in the centre, and cavalry on both wings, with Cromwell on the Parliamentary right wing. Immediately, Cromwell sent a regiment of dragoons (heavy cavalry that could dismount and fight as infantry), into the hedges, where they dismounted and began firing on the advancing Royalists.

The Battle

As the Royalists attacked, Rupert's cavalry matched the pace of the infantry. Fairfax's infantry advanced to meet them but were pushed back and began losing ground. His cavalry rushed to aid the hard-pressed foot soldiers, driving back Rupert's front rank and turning to charge the Royalist infantry. Ranks of Royalist pikes brought a halt to the horsemen, as Rupert's second line charged and drove them from the field. They fled 24 kilometres (15 miles) to Northampton, with Rupert in hot pursuit.

This left Cromwell and the Northern Horse in deadlock on the opposite wing, since whoever went to help their infantry first risked being charged in turn. After half an hour, the outnumbered Royalists charged up a slope encumbered with bushes and rabbit holes. Cromwell sent forward a third of his force to rout them, leaving the remainder free to sweep round the Royalist left wing to attack their infantry from the rear. At the same time, the dragoons on the opposite flank could now remount and attack the Royalist infantry from the other side.

The Outcome and Significance

The result was inevitable. Some Royalist infantry surrendered, others fought to the bitter end. By the time Rupert rallied his men and returned to the battle after failing to capture Fairfax's baggage train, the day was lost. Fairfax recaptured Leicester and marched into the West Country to defeat the Royalists there. Defeat at Naseby ended all Charles's hopes of victory. His best troops were lost and the enemy captured letters showing that he had begged for help from Catholics in Ireland and Europe. When these were published, his support waned and Parliamentary victory ended the first Civil War a year later.

Naseby had proved the value of using tougher, better-trained professional troops to deliver a decisive punch when ordered. With them rose the threat of military dictatorship, as Cromwell's New Model Army became more difficult for even Parliament to control, forcing its successors to operate under closer political command ever after.

Tactics of Deception

Where:	Blenheim, Bavaria, Germany
When:	1704
War:	War of the Spanish Succession (1701–1714)
Combatants:	England and Austria vs. France and Bavaria
Casualties:	English and Austrians: 4,500; French and allies: 9,000

In 1704, the Duke of Marlborough mounted a brilliant deception to enable his British army to intercept and defeat a French attempt to attack Vienna during the War of the Spanish Succession. By the early-18th century, wars often involved complex alliances. To prevent the French inheriting the Spanish Empire on the death of the Spanish monarch Charles II, the Dutch, English, Danes, Austrians and Prussians were fighting the French and their Bavarian allies. Marlborough had to relieve French pressure on Vienna, while reassuring the Dutch that they would not be left exposed to French attacks in turn.

Given Dutch agreement to march to the Moselle, a tributary of the Rhine, Marlborough wanted to continue to join his Austrian allies at Donauworth on the Danube, 400 kilometres (250 miles) away, to block a French march on Vienna. He deceived the French that he intended to attack in Alsace, by building bridges of boats across the Rhine at Philippsburg, which he never used, while moving his army upriver on barges, covering 130 kilometres (80 miles) a day. The French forces threatening the Netherlands set off in pursuit, leaving the Dutch secure enough to send him reinforcements. Finally heading across country, Marlborough reached the Danube five weeks later on 22 June 1704, free for the summer campaign against the Bavarians.

The Positions

Finally realizing their mistake, the French rushed after the Duke of Marlborough. At the beginning of August, the approach of the French army under Marshal Tallard led Marlborough and Prince Eugene, his Austrian ally,

Above The Battle of Blenheim. The dismounted 2nd North British Dragoons, under Marlborough and Prince Eugene, storm the village and defeat the French and Bavarians.

to form a strong defensive position near the village of Blenheim on the north bank of the Danube, west of Donauworth in Germany, with Eugene's Austrians on his right, to bar the French from Vienna.

Facing them on 13 August was Tallard's army, with the Bavarians on his left flank, a total of 56,000 men against Marlborough's 52,000 but the British general had trained his cavalry as carefully as Cromwell (see page 32) to dominate the battlefield through shock action, charging with swords rather than pistols and carbines. Where French infantry charged with the bayonet, Marlborough knew that timed and aimed volleys could deliver a blow no enemy could withstand. His small and manoeuvereable infantry formations were trained to let the enemy fire first, while loading and aiming with care for a devastating counterpunch. His final deception suggested he would fall back to the north-east if the French attacked. British soldiers captured by French patrols relayed this rumour, so that Marlborough's attack came as a complete surprise.

The Battle

Marlborough knew that his enemy's weakest point was the junction between French and Bavarian formations. To distract their attention, he ordered Eugene to attack the Bavarians on Tallard's left, while he attacked the enemy's opposite flank, centred on the village of Blenheim. It was a gamble, as fierce Bavarian counterattacks were soon driving Eugene's men back; they also beat back two strong assaults on the strongpoint of Blenheim. Yet the French had been forced to divert heavy reinforcements in order to defend the position.

Consequently Tallard's centre was growing steadily weaker. Finally, Marlborough ordered his centre to advance. Seven battalions of infantry, followed by 72 squadrons of cavalry, were supported by another 11 battalions of infantry following behind. When enemy fire stopped the leading files of infantry, they opened up gaps to let the cavalry through. Desperate, the French horsemen beat back the initial charge but the British infantry, firing their deliberate volleys, cut the opposing ranks to pieces. As their cohesion crumbled, Marlborough's cavalry charged into the widening gap. The enemy line was cut in two and Marlborough's horsemen wheeled left to drive their shattered and demoralized troops into the river.

The Outcome and Significance

Blenheim was fiercely fought, with heavy casualties. Tallard was captured and his last 10,000 troops surrendered. It was a decisive victory, at a cost of 30,000 French casualties and 14,000 prisoners: the victors had lost 4,500 killed and 8,000 wounded. Bavaria became part of the Austrian Empire and Marlborough won additional victories at Ramillies and Oudenarde before changes at home brought his recall. The war ended in 1714 with neither side winning decisively.

French infantry tactics using bayonet charges for shock action would be developed to battle-winning effect by Napoleon a century later, where Marlborough's riposte of timed and accurately aimed volleys would also find its ultimate expression in Wellington's army. From Spain and Portugal to Waterloo, British doggedness would match, and finally defeat, French elan. Yet the irony of Blenheim was that Marlborough's skill at moving his forces hundreds of miles to concentrate when needed to inflict a decisive defeat would provide an inspiration for Napoleon himself.

Prussian Speed and Discipline

Where: Leuthen, Prussian Silesia, now
           Lutyniya in Poland
When: 1757
War: Seven Years' War (1756–1763)
Combatants: Prussia vs. Austria
Casualties: Prussians: 1,100;
           Austrians: 3,000

In 1759, Frederick the Great's ferociously disciplined Prussian Army marched 270 kilometres (170 miles) in 12 days after beating one enemy army to defeat another that threatened his province of Silesia. Frederick had turned his country into a major military power by building the largest possible army, and spending four-fifths of the country's wealth on it. Citizens served for years under poor pay and ferocious discipline, but were drilled to perfection. His soldiers could load and fire five shots a minute where most other armies could manage two or three. Muskets could be loaded, aimed and fired with bayonets fixed, so charges could be made immediately after firing a devastating volley.

The Positions

On 5 November 1757, Frederick beat the French and Austrians at Rossbach near Bonn, only to hear on 28 November, that a second Austrian army had taken Breslau (now Wroclaw in Poland). He marched his army 270 kilometres (170 miles) to approach the city on 5 December, where he found the enemy waiting at the village of Leuthen, 16 kilometres (10 miles) to the west. Not only did they have 72,000 men to his own 45,000 but their line was over 6 kilometres (4 miles) long, rendering his favourite tactic – outflanking the enemy – impossible. Nevertheless the area had been a training ground for Frederick's troops and he knew it well.

The Battle

First Frederick launched a number of his cavalry to threaten the Austrian right flank. Then he formed his infantry into columns, screened by his remaining cavalry and marched them southwards behind a range of low hills towards the Austrian left flank. Convinced this was a prudent Prussian retreat from superior numbers, the Austrian commander decided it was safe to move his reserves towards his apparently threatened right flank.

It was a fatal mistake. Frederick's 43,000 infantry marched past the end of the Austrian line, towing one 6-pounder cannon with each battalion and reinforced by a full battery of ten 12-pounder guns and then they wheeled to the left and into line. Ironically, the proximity of the hills that hid Frederick's move had encouraged the Austrians to place their least experienced troops there and they now faced the onslaught.

The combination of Prussian infantry steadily advancing with devastating volley fire, backed up by mobile artillery, proved irresistible. Frederick sent his battalions marching in a diagonal formation 45 metres (147 feet) apart, a manoeuvre first used by the Spartan general, Epaminondas, in 369 BCE. The increasing pressure caused the Austrian line to break from left to right as the full weight of the Prussian guns, rifles and cavalry began to tell.

Desperately the Austrians swung their line around to meet the Prussians, but over such a long front, some units took an hour and a half to reform. By then the Prussians had taken Leuthen at the Austrian centre. The Austrian cavalry tried charging the Prussian infantry, but a massive Prussian countercharge drove them back behind their own lines. It was enough: after three hours, Frederick had won a decisive victory.

The Outcome and Significance

Silesia remained in Prussian hands. Yet Frederick became a victim of his own self-belief. Increasingly bloody battles left his country weakened by huge casualties. Only by staying on the defensive did he survive to the end of the war in 1763.

Many experts believed that Frederick's attack in diagonal formation had been decisive, though he never used this tactic again on a large scale. The truly decisive factor had been using mobile guns. The tactic of a rapid advance with mobile artillery keeping pace was the ancestor of the German blitzkrieg of 1940 (see page 82).

Riflemen Overcome Regular Army

Where: Cowpens, South Carolina, USA
When: 1781
War: American War of Independence
              (1775–1783)
Combatants: Britain vs. America
Casualties: British: 110; Americans: 25

In January 1781, the US General Daniel Morgan, led an army into South Carolina to raise the locals against British regulars under Lieutenant Colonel Banastre Tarleton. Most American militiamen used hunting rifles with spiral grooves inside the barrel to impart a spin to the ball as it was fired; this greatly improved its accuracy for aimed shots rather than massed volleys. Their stealth and accuracy at the Cowpens helped defeat regular British infantry.

The Positions

On 16 January, Morgan's force was chased by Tarleton to the crossroads and pastures of the Cowpens, where local militia had gathered. Local loyalists described Morgan's position in open parkland, ideal for Tarleton's dragoons. He arrived at the Cowpens in a misty dawn with infantry and artillery flanked by dragoons on either side. Morgan hid his militia riflemen under cover as an advance guard, with more militia in a line behind them and a third line of regular American troops. Immediately, Tarleton ordered 50 dragoons to attack.

The Battle

The riflemen's fire proved deadly, cutting down more than one-third of the dragoons, and forcing the rest to fall back. Tarleton ordered half his infantry to advance, escorted by dragoons, and they drove the militia back. Tarleton thought the battle was won and ordered his dragoons to chase the retreating militia. This allowed Morgan's reserve force of American cavalry to charge out of cover and drive the dragoons back in turn. Tarleton reformed his infantry and sent them against the right flank of the rearmost line of enemy troops. These were American regulars, trained to fire volleys and a bloody duel followed.

Tarleton now sent the rest of his infantry to outflank the right of the American line. To prevent this, the right flank troops fell back, which the British thought was an American retreat. However, the British charged forward, only to find the Americans moving to a prepared position, before turning and firing a single, crippling volley, which they followed up with a bayonet charge. This was regular against regular and fortunes changed in an instant. The British fell back or surrendered at bayonet point. The militia attacked from one side and the regulars from the other, overwhelming the British between them. Tarleton's reserve cavalry refused to charge and he had to escape. The battle was over after little more than an hour.

The Outcome and Significance

Victory greatly heartened the rebel cause, though, and by September Lord Cornwallis and his army were confined in Yorktown by French and American troops, ferried aboard French ships. On 17 October, the British surrendered and the rebels had finally won their independence.

The British soon trained their own sharpshooters to fire accurately from cover, armed with rifles and clad in drab dark-green uniforms. The 95th Rifles and the 60th Rifles, formed originally from loyalists as the Royal Americans, would soon be joined by soldiers everywhere in wearing camouflaged uniforms and firing rifles instead of muskets.

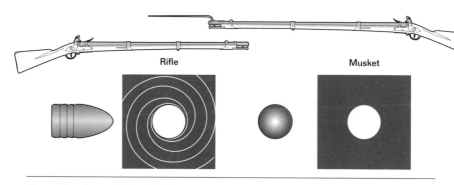

Rifle

Musket

Above View down the barrel of the militiamen's rifle; the spiralled rifling made the bullet spin, providing greater accuracy than the musket's smooth barrel and round ball.

Advent of Mass Warfare

Where: Valmy, eastern France
When: 1792
War: French Revolutionary War
         (1792–1802)
Combatants: France vs. Prussia
Casualties: French: 300; Prussians: 184

The speed and violence of the French Revolution of 1789 terrified European monarchies. Quickly they prepared to crush the rebels before the contagion could spread to their own subjects. Completely undaunted by the odds, on 20 April 1792, France declared war on Austria. This effrontery resulted in an army of 35,000 – Austrians, Hessians and Prussians – crossing the French border on 19 August, commanded by the Duke of Brunswick. It advanced slowly, taking the eastern French fortresses of Longwy and Verdun before heading for Paris. Two French Revolutionary armies of eager volunteers with a core of old soldiers from the former Royal army, rushed to bar its way.

The Positions
Brunswick's army was entering the narrow valleys and steep hills of the Argonne Forest when the French Army of the North, commanded by Charles François Dumouriez, arrived from the Netherlands to block their route. Crossing in front of the Prussian advance guard, his men reached the Paris road first. They were badly outnumbered and General François Christophe Kellermann, with the French Army of the Centre, was marching from Metz to reinforce them but his troops were still on the way when the Prussian attack began.

The Battle
Brunswick began by forcing back the northern part of Dumouriez' line. Instead of retreating, the French commander simply moved his left wing back and wheeled his troops to face north instead of east. Kellermann arrived with his troops on 20 September, bringing the French numbers to 47,000.

Brunswick began outflanking the French left to cut them off from the Paris road. Kellermann, commanding in Dumouriez' temporary absence at a better vantage point, moved his men forward to a line from the village of Sainte Menehould to an old mill at Valmy, north of the Paris road but still blocking the Prussians' route. At last, the Prussian columns began advancing, and the French played their remaining trump card: their artillery.

During the twilight years of the French monarchy, de Gribeauval, the army Inspector General, had standardized guns of lighter construction for easier handling, with improved sights for greater accuracy. This had made French artillery the most formidable in Europe and the results were soon plain to see. French fire broke up the Prussian columns and the infantry fell back. The French infantry held their ground and cheered, and this demonstration of defiance, allied to the accurate barrage, brought about the repulse of a second attack. Finally, the attackers withdrew out of range and fighting petered out. The French suffered 300 casualties and the Prussians and their allies 184, a trifling loss for such a momentous battle.

The Outcome and Significance

News echoed across Europe. The next day, the French abolished their monarchy. After 10 days, the Prussians and their allies, sick from dysentery, withdrew from French soil. New French armies were soon fighting victorious engagements in Belgium, Germany and Savoy before growing international opposition raised the stakes.

The significance of the skirmish at Valmy far outweighs its apparent triviality, where the dash of French Revolutionary volunteers beat back a trained professional army. The battle spawned new French tactics, as universal conscription paved the way for mass warfare and the huge national armies of the two world wars. Because they lacked supplies and equipment, these new armies marched fast and lightly equipped. Unable to deploy in the complex formations of conventional battle, they became expert at sniping from cover until their opponents faltered, whereupon they would rise en masse and attack at the decisive moment. Usually they triumphed and in another decade these tactics would be perfected by Napoleon.

Speed and Mobility

Where: Austerlitz, present-day Czech
              Republic
When: 1805
War: Napoleonic War (1803–1815)
Combatants: France vs. Austria and Russia
Casualties: French: 1,305;
              Austro-Russians: 3,000

Already two coalitions between countries striving to limit the rise of French power had been broken by Napoleon's invasion of the Tyrol in 1797 and by the Treaty of Amiens in 1802. Now, although Nelson's victory at Trafalgar (see page 114) had dashed Napoleon's hopes of invading England, Britain's partners in the Third Coalition, Sweden, Austria and Russia, were marching against him. Even before his fleet had been destroyed, Napoleon had sent his invasion army across the Rhine on 25 September to face the Austrians and Russians.

Marshal Mack's Austrian army was waiting in the fortress of Ulm on the Danube in southern Germany for their Russian allies. Mack sent out two large columns to find the French. On October 14 one column ran into Marshal Ney and the VI Corps of Napoleon's army and was defeated. Meanwhile the rest of Napoleon's troops were wheeling northwards to appear behind Mack's positions, forcing him to surrender six days later.

The Positions

Too late to save Ulm, the Russians retreated eastwards to allow surviving Austrian units to join them. By the time Napoleon caught up, they were 110 kilometres (70 miles) north of Vienna, astride a range of snow-covered hills near the village of Austerlitz, east of Brno in what is now the Czech Republic. Napoleon needed to win decisively, while Austria still reeled from Ulm and before Prussia could join the forces arrayed against him. On 1 December, the eve of the battle, he faced around 50,000 Russians with 23,000 Austrians and 318 guns. So far, Napoleon had assembled 68,000 troops, with another 7,000 under Marshal Davout, who was rushing from Vienna to join him.

The Battle

Napoleon wanted to tempt the enemy to attack his right wing, by moving troops away from it. This would allow him to launch a powerful attack against his opponent's centre on the Pratzen Heights, which dominated the battlefield. Exactly on cue, the enemy marched on his right wing with five massive infantry columns totalling almost 60,000 men, to cut the French off from Vienna. At the same time, they launched a second attack along the high road to Brno against the French left flank. After this double blow, a final attack in the centre should complete their envelopment and destruction.

Soldiers say no plan ever survives contact with the enemy and this was no exception. The enemy infantry marched against the French right wing at dawn on 2 December. Making their way through the early morning fog, they found themselves barred by the 11th-hour arrival of Davout's reinforcements. More troops had to be sent across the French front from the Pratzen Heights to join the attack. Napoleon saw his opportunity at 09.00 and seized it. He sent Marshal Soult's corps to attack the enemy's weakened centre and exposed flank. Conditions were still misty, adding the advantage of surprise and, by 11.00, the heights were in French hands.

At 13.00, the Russian Imperial Guard tried to recapture the high ground. Napoleon committed his own reserves, including the French Imperial Guard cavalry. After bitter fighting, the French drove back the Russians and secured their position, leaving Soult free to swing to his right and attack the rear of those enemy formations still attacking the French right wing. These now began to retreat, some crossing the frozen Satschan lakes, but the French used artillery to break the ice, causing many to drown in the freezing water. Ironically, the French had been driven back at the opposite end of their front, but as the allied line melted away, the pressure here finally eased.

The Outcome and Significance

Austerlitz was a decisive French victory. The enemy lost 12,200 killed and wounded, 133 guns and 15,000 prisoners while Napoleon's army lost some 6,800 casualties, most on the threatened right wing where at one point they had faced, and defeated, odds of four to one. Austria asked for terms and Russia withdrew, leaving England fighting alone until joined by Prussia in 1806.

The battle had been a perfect demonstration of Napoleonic variations on French Revolutionary tactics. This was the high point of his career, with his tactics of rapid manoeuvre, speedy concentration, and devastating attack. He perfected the art of splitting his armies into smaller groups marching and living off the countryside, following different routes to their ultimate objective and inflicting defeats like Elchingen on the way. Only when they finally assembled to deliver a knockout blow would his demoralized enemy realize what was happening. Unfortunately, his increasing ambition made his victories more expensive, while his opponents developed countertactics to bring about his downfall.

Right Napoleon Bonaparte, military and political leader of France, 20 March 1804 to 6 April 1814, and 1 March 1815 to 22 June 1815.

Defence in Depth

Where: Torres Vedras, Portugal
When: 1810–11
War: Napoleonic War (1803–1815)
Combatants: Britain vs. France
Casualties: British: almost none;
              French: 20,000

Napoleon's fast, mobile warfare met new problems when he invaded Spain and Portugal in an attempt to place his brother Joseph on the Spanish throne. Guerrilla attacks prevented light formations from moving to a timetable. Even a single message needed a heavy cavalry escort throughout its journey, and supply lines were long and fragile. Worse, in a sparse countryside of burned villages and crops, troops could not live off the barren winter landscape. Meanwhile Wellington, commanding the British army, was supplied by sea, and paid for local goods in order to retain the support of the population. But he was still vulnerable to outflanking by two more French armies, and as he retreated into Portugal, he needed a secure winter base.

The Positions

With Portuguese help, he fortified the Tagus peninsula some 40 kilometres (25 miles) north of Lisbon, an ideal defensive position, impossible to outflank and with perfect access to the sea. From November 1809 to September 1810, surveyors and workmen designed and built the Lines of Torres Vedras – two successive barriers of 87 fortifications and batteries armed with 290 guns, across the entire peninsula. Small redoubts, each holding 200 men with three light artillery pieces, were sited on the crests of ridges, close enough to give support to one another if attacked. Slopes were blasted to make sheer cliffs, while olive trees blocked any gullies, making them impossible to advance through but easy to sweep with grapeshot. Dams flooded wide areas, and all possible cover – buildings, vineyards and olive groves – was removed. Semaphores sent messages the length of the lines in minutes and new military roads allowed rapid troop movement. Finally, the local population, with crops and animals, were brought into the lines, leaving the French to advance into a desert.

The Battle

Tight security left the French completely surprised. When Marshal Massena and his 61,000 men approached on 15 October 1810, intending to drive the British into the sea, he met a powerful series of defences. His men took one small redoubt but failed against a larger and more heavily defended position; he was forced to retire to a safe distance. Napoleon ordered a blockade of the lines, to prevent supplies reaching the British, a possibility inland but fruitless so close to the sea. Massena and his men stayed for five weeks, through one of Portugal's coldest winters, short of food and even firewood. The British and Portuguese remained safe, healthy, warm and well fed without having to fight a battle. Instead the French had to fight cold, hunger and disease – opponents who suffered no casualties and who gave them no quarter.

The Outcome and Significance

On 15 November, with his men starving, sick and harried by guerrillas, Massena disobeyed his emperor and retreated across the Spanish frontier until the spring. In all he lost 20,000 men, a third of his force, the price of a major defeat, though barely a shot had been fired. The brilliance of Wellington's defences had rendered Napoleon's tactics powerless. In 1811, Wellington's rested and reinforced army emerged from the lines and never had to return. They finally marched on to French soil in 1814, as their allies approached from the east. The French surrender led to Napoleon's exile to Elba, his dramatic return and the end at Waterloo.

In the harsh conditions of Spain and Portugal, Wellington found the counter to Napoleonic tactics, turning siege warfare around so that the besieged British lived well while the French besiegers starved. The sharpest lessons of Torres Vedras were that the best battles are won without a fight; that naval support changes the rules of land fighting; and that defence in depth remains the strongest counter to wars of movement, a truth enduring today.

Frontal Attacks Prove Costly

Where: Borodino, west of Moscow, Russia
When: 1812
War: Napoleonic War (1803–1815)
Combatants: France vs. Russia
Casualties: French: 7,000; Russian: 9,000

Napoleon's tactics were growing increasingly dependent on bloody frontal attacks, costing losses he could not afford, especially on his hopelessly ambitious invasion of Russia in 1812. Fast mobile warfare was unsuited to the vast distances the French crossed on the road to Moscow, and they failed to force their opponents to battle. Meanwhile, hunger and disease thinned their ranks, and Napoleon needed a victory to put Russia out of the fight before the winter. Finally, his chance came when the Russian commander, General Kutusov, made a stand with 120,000 men and 640 guns at Borodino, 120 kilometres (75 miles) from Moscow and the last naturally defensive position before the capital.

The Positions

Kutusov's position around the village of Borodino was based on the massive Raevski redoubt, an open-backed earthwork containing nineteen 12-pounder cannons. His right flank rested on the Moskva river and his line followed its steeply-banked Kolocha tributary to the village of Utitza. The heavily wooded far bank of the Kolocha would hamper the deployment of French attacks, while three arrow-headed redoubts, called fleches, defended the exposed Russian left flank. Casualties and sickness had cut French numbers down from 250,000 men to 133,000 with 587 guns. Marshal Davout spotted the relatively weak Russian right wing and wanted to make a flank attack, but Napoleon refused, ordering a frontal attack instead.

The Battle

Fighting began at 06.00, with an enormous barrage from the 102-gun French main battery. Two French divisions attacked the arrowhead redoubts, but as they emerged from the wooded riverbank, Russian batteries pounded them from the higher ground by the village of Semyanovskaya. Their losses mounted but after an hour and a half they captured all three redoubts. A Russian counterattack threw them back again, until a second French attack retook the positions. This threatened the Semyanovskaya battery so the Russians reinforced it with 24 more guns.

Late in the morning, the French cavalry passed the redoubts to attack oncoming Russian infantry. Russian cuirassiers charged them in turn, forcing them back. In the meantime, the French artillery battered the oncoming Russian infantry but thick smoke clouds hid their confusion and vulnerability. Napoleon refused calls for reinforcements, keeping the Imperial Guard as his last reserve. Meanwhile the French captured the village of Borodino and were thrown back by Russian attacks before retaking it once more. By early afternoon most of the French were across the Kalocha river and their guns were pounding the Raevsky redoubt, which fell soon afterwards. The Russians then brought up three more batteries of horse artillery to shell the redoubt and retake it.

Both sides' artillery imposed a terrible slaughter. At 14.00 Napoleon ordered another massive attack on the Raevsky redoubt. French artillery shattered Russian infantry moving up to counterattack, while Russian musketry turned back French cavalry trying to recapture the redoubt. Finally, the French took the position for the last time. Both sides were so exhausted that only the artillery still fired.

The Outcome and Significance

Following the battle, the Russians moved back to regroup, abandoning Moscow to the French, but a surrender was never agreed. Fire swept the city and shortage of supplies forced a terrible retreat. Only 40,000 French soldiers finally reached safety after a nightmare march through snowstorms and Cossack attacks.

Napoleon's victory ensured he lost the campaign. His costly and uninspired tactics showed his inspiration had run out, and Borodino remains a monument to the fearful cost of frontal attacks against strong defences. During a week's fighting between Germans and Russians in 1941 – with all the power of modern weapons – casualties were lower than on that single day's fighting on the same spot 129 years earlier.

A Linear Defence

Where: Waterloo, south of Brussels,
              Belgium
When: 1815
War: Napoleonic War (1803–1815)
Combatants: Britain and Prussia vs. France
Casualties: British and Prussians: 4,000;
              French: 5,000–15,000

Napoleon escaped from Elba to France in March 1815. His army reformed, while England, Austria, Prussia and Russia strove to depose him. Only a decisive victory offered Napoleon any hope, which meant defeating his enemies in turn. Closest were the Duke of Wellington in southern Belgium with an Anglo-Dutch army of 93,000 and Field Marshal Blücher with 116,000 Prussians. With 124,000 of his own troops, Napoleon might beat them one at a time.

The Positions

By 15 June 1815, Napoleon's army was close enough to drive between Wellington and Blücher. He attacked the Prussians the next day, leaving Marshal Ney to push back the British at Quatre Bras, south of Waterloo, before wheeling right to complete the Prussians' destruction and then deal with Wellington. The French began by inflicting 12,000 Prussian casualties for 8,000 of their own but Blücher's army was far from destroyed. Early the next day, Wellington avoided encirclement by retreating to Waterloo. There he massed his army along the Mont St. Jean ridge across the main road to Brussels. In the centre, he fortified a walled farm, La Haye Sainte, and on his right the chateau, garden and walled orchard of Hougoumont. He placed riflemen in a nearby sand quarry and protected his left flank by the fortified hamlet of Papelotte. He hid most remaining infantry from artillery behind the crest line, a tactic he had used in Spain.

The Battle

Early on 18 June, Napoleon sent Marshal Grouchy with a third of his army to pursue the Prussians to the east. Then, at almost midday, he ordered his artillery to attack the British centre, La Haye Sainte. His troops then attacked Hougoumont. British artillery beat back the first assault and the Guards the second, before holding the position. Both commanders realized its vital importance, and sent massed troops to fight for it.

At 13.00 Napoleon saw Prussians in the distance. He sent orders to recall Grouchy but by this time the latter had gone too far to return in time. Defeating Wellington was now urgent, so Napoleon sent in 14,000 infantry in massive columns on either side of La Haye Sainte. For a time, the massed fire of 6,000 British infantry

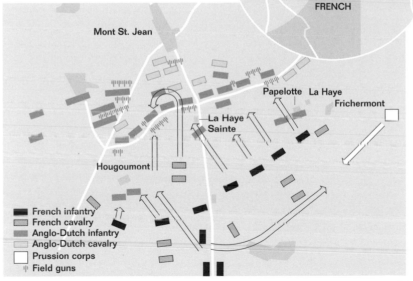

Above French, British and Prussian movements and positions at the Battle of Waterloo.

held them back, but numbers began to tell, until two brigades of British heavy horse charged the enemy. The British cavalry shattered the French attack but were countercharged by more French cuirassiers and lancers and losses were heavy on both sides. Yet the Prussians were now much closer and events were slipping out of Napoleon's control.

At 16.00, a huge French cavalry attack forced the British infantry to form compact squares, presenting even charging horsemen with a hedge of bayonets and massed volleys to deflect their attacks. Even when the French sent in their last reserves, some 9,000 horsemen, the squares stood firm. Then La Haye Sainte finally fell after its defenders ran out of ammunition. The French brought up horse artillery and hammered the British squares with canister.

Both commanders were almost out of options. Prussians were outflanking Napoleon's right and threatening his retreat as they bent back the French line into a horseshoe curve. At 19.30, Napoleon threw his last reserve – the Imperial Guard – at the British centre. The columns of the Old Guard had won battles all over Europe but British artillery and cavalry now broke their first formation. The second was stopped by disciplined point-blank volleys from the Guards, then a bayonet charge to rout the survivors. The third column drove the Guards back but British light infantry lined up on their flank to fire volleys into their ranks, shattering this last French hope.

The Outcome and Significance

The battle was effectively over, though isolated French units fought to the end. The Prussians lost 15,000 and Wellington 7,000 but the French lost 40,000 including prisoners. One casualty was Napoleon's dream of empire – ahead lay imprisonment on the remote island of St. Helena, where he died in 1821.

Waterloo represented the final supremacy of British tactics of linear defence with aimed volleys of musketry against the shock tactics of Napoleon's advancing columns. The battle ended the supremacy of Napoleon's light and mobile tactics, defeated by British sea power, alliances of his opponents and his own mistakes. Even at Waterloo, he failed to deploy all his troops and ignored his three best commanders – one barred by his own disapproval, one serving in an office and the third on a distant frontier far from the fighting.

Napoleonic Tactics in America

Where: Chancellorsville, Virginia, USA
When: 1863
War: American Civil War (1861–65)
Combatants: Confederates vs. Union
Casualties: Confederates: 1,665; Union: 1,606

The American Civil War cost the lives of 500,000 American soldiers, more than any war before or since. Since Napoleon's time, weapons had greater range and accuracy and could be reloaded more quickly, making attacks far more costly, so troops could only survive protected by trenches and earthworks. The Union North had all the advantages: twice the population, most of the experienced professionals and most of the industry. Yet Confederate Southerners were as skilled at hunting and living off the land as their Revolutionary War forebears. Under General Robert E. Lee, the South won a vital victory at Fredericksburg, Virginia, in 1862. In late April 1863, the North was seeking revenge.

The Positions

The Northern Army of the Potomac, under Major General Joseph Hooker, crossed the Rappahannock River on either side of the Southern position at Fredericksburg to catch Lee's army in a huge pincer movement. However, once Lee's cavalry warned his right flank was exposed, he decided to attack rather than fall back to avoid the trap.

It was a colossal gamble: Lee's 55,000-strong army was outnumbered more than two to one but he had four important advantages. The Northern right wing was advancing through the Spotsylvania Wilderness, an almost trackless forest that gave little chance to use their artillery. Local knowledge and stealth would be decisive. With numbers so heavily against him, Lee's opponents would not expect an attack and most Northern cavalry had gone far to the east to cut Southern supply routes, so he would know little about Southern positions and movements.

The Battle

On 2 May, Lee sent 26,000 troops under 'Stonewall' Jackson to outflank the Northern right flank. To distract the enemy, Lee used 17,000 of his remaining troops to threaten an attack against their centre at Chancellorsville, where they waited for reinforcements. Brief sightings of Jackson's troops convinced the enemy they were retreating. One Union corps fought Jackson's rearguard at Catharine Furnace but by then Jackson's leading troops were miles ahead and the battle drew off more men from the already weakened right flank.

Finally, at 17.00 the 11,000 Union soldiers remaining on the right flank were cooking their dinner when 11 brigades of Jackson's troops hit them in a surprise attack. In spite of orders, they had dug no defences. Jackson captured more than one-third without firing a shot, while pushing the rest back more than 3 kilometres (2 miles) to Chancellorsville. The leading Northern troops then pulled back to avoid encirclement, allowing Jackson and Lee to join up and occupy a clearing on higher ground, called Hazel Grove, ideal for artillery. That night, Jackson was returning to camp when a sentry mistakenly shot him; he died a week later. His replacement, Jeb Stuart, began shelling the Northern positions from Hazel Grove. In the evening another Southern attack captured Chancellorsville and left Union troops holding a ford across the river as their only line of retreat.

The Outcome and Significance

On 3 May, Hooker attacked the rear of Lee's army. Delays enabled Lee to stop the attack and push the Northerners back, in a struggle where many wounded died when the dense woodland caught fire. On 4 May, Hooker stayed on the defensive. The Confederates pushed his left wing back across Banks' Ford early the following day. As this crossing was needed for Hooker's army to attack Lee further downstream, his only option was retreat. The South had won another important victory.

Napoleonic tactics of stealth and movement had proved effective in the very different conditions of the American Civil War. Lee's tactics seized victory from the jaws of defeat, but arithmetic was against him. Both sides suffered heavy losses but the price was higher for Lee's much smaller army, and the balance would tilt further in favour of the Union.

Fortified Positions

Where: Gettysburg, Pennsylvania, USA
When: 1863
War: American Civil War (1861–65)
Combatants: Confederates vs. Union
Casualties: Confederates: 4,700; Union: 3,200

Following the defeat at Chancellorsville (see page 53), General George Meade, with 97,000 men, spent the summer of 1863 searching for his Southern opponent, General Robert E. Lee, and his 75,000 strong Army of Northern Virginia. Lee was then marching into Pennsylvania to destroy the strategic rail bridge at Harrisburg, before turning east to raise the Union siege of the Southern fortress of Vicksburg, and threaten Baltimore, Philadelphia, or even Washington itself. His troops would also find living off the land easier in the richer countryside of the North than in the impoverished land of Virginia.

On 30 June, an advance brigade of Lee's army approached the Pennsylvania town of Gettysburg from the north, searching for supplies. To their surprise, they spotted Union cavalry on McPherson Ridge, a mile to the west. They brought reinforcements and returned the following day to attack the Union soldiers. In bitter fighting, the Union cavalry held firm long enough for reinforcements to help them push the Southerners back. Then more Southern troops arrived and pushed the now outnumbered Union force back through the town in a bitter delaying action. Nevertheless, thousands were captured before the rest took up a much more secure position on Cemetery Ridge to the south of Gettysburg.

The Positions

As more troops rushed to the scene, both armies raced to build fortifications. By the morning of 2 July, it was clear the Union army's lines on Cemetery Ridge and the slopes to the south were closely paralleled by Confederate positions on Seminary Ridge almost a mile to the west. At the northern end of both ridges, the Union line swung round to the right in a 'fish-hook' formation, with the Confederate lines following a parallel curve. The weapons of the time meant both armies could only make an attack by descending from the safety of the crests into the low ground separating the two lines and then charging uphill into heavy fire.

The Battle

Lee began by attacking both Union flanks. The Union right beat the Confederates back when they tried to capture Culp's Hill and East Cemetery Ridge. Communications were poor: had Lee's men been reinforced by troops from within Gettysburg itself, or had they known how close was the vulnerable Northern supply train, they might have been more successful. On the Union left, Lee's men broke through their lines, pushing the enemy back towards an unoccupied hill called Little Round Top. Here, too, they missed an opportunity as the enemy quickly took over this vital position.

On 3 July, Lee's inspiration seemed to desert him, as had Napoleon's more than 50 years before. Held up on both flanks, he ordered a frontal assault on the strong enemy centre at Cemetery Ridge. At 13.00, Southern guns began pounding Union positions but they were running short of ammunition and the Union troops were so well dug in that little damage was done. Next, 15,000 Confederate soldiers under General George E. Pickett marched forward under heavy fire from artillery and riflemen and charged up Cemetery Ridge.

The result was inevitable. In less than an hour, two-thirds of the Confederate attackers were killed or wounded and Pickett's Charge had failed. Lee could make no more attacks and on the following afternoon, 4 July, his army began marching south towards Virginia. Meade was praised for his victory but criticized for not pursuing Lee more vigorously, though there was no doubt Gettysburg was a genuine victory.

The Outcome and Significance

Lee's defeat ended the second Southern attempt to invade Northern territory. His attack plan had been based on poor intelligence, caused by the absence of cavalry, and he seemed to fall victim to the belief that his army was invincible after earlier victories. Nevertheless, he managed to elude his pursuers, aided by Meade's shortage of cavalry horses and the fact that many Union soldiers

had to march barefoot because of shortages of supplies. The siege of
Vicksburg ended in a Southern surrender on the day of Lee's defeat. More
ominously, Confederate hopes of a negotiated end to the war were dashed,
as Union attitudes hardened. Two more years of war would lead to the
inevitable final defeat.

Lee's Napoleonic tactics, which won the battle of Chancellorsville, gave
way to Napoleonic failings at the battle of Gettysburg, where frontal attacks
at strong Northern positions failed catastrophically. Warfare was becoming
more industrial, with numbers and firepower counting more heavily against
fighting spirit and inspired tactics and the heavily fortified positions at
Gettysburg had defeated Lee's ingenuity as they would defeat the Germans on
the Western Front 50 years later.

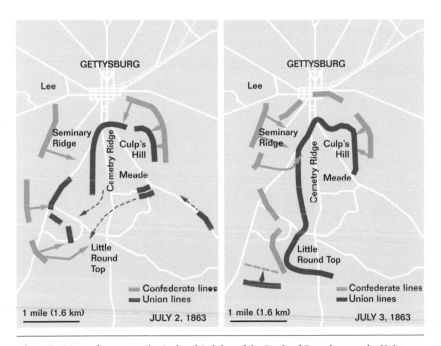

Above Positions of troops on the 2nd and 3rd day of the Battle of Gettysburg as the Union
'fish hook' position formed.

Part Three:

Wars of Empire

Numerical Advantage Overturned

Where: Plassey, Bengal, India
When: 1757
War: Seven Years' War (1756–63)
Combatants: East India Company vs.
            Nawab of Bengal
Casualties: East India Company: 22;
            Nawab of Bengal: 100

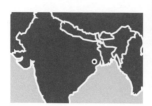

Some battles carry significance far beyond their immediate relevence or the numbers involved. In April 1756, Britain's East India Company was threatened by the accession of a new Nawab of Bengal. The 26 year-old Siraj-ud-Daulah was sympathetic to the Company's French rivals, who had begun training his soldiers to operate heavy artillery. As part of his reforms, the Nawab dismissed his grand uncle Mir Jafar as army commander.

In June 1756, he captured the British base of Fort William in Calcutta. The East India Company reacted by sending troops from its base at Madras under Robert Clive, a former company clerk with no military training, who had successfully defended British interests in southern India. Clive recaptured Fort William on 2 January 1757. As pressure from the French-backed Nawab increased, the British were finally provoked into an attempt to replace him with Mir Jafar.

The Positions

In June 1757, Clive marched from Calcutta to the Nawab's capital of Murshidabad and on 21 June his army of 1,100 European and 2,100 Indian soldiers reached the mango groves of Plassey, during the first downpour of the monsoon. There they faced the Nawab's army of 50,000 infantry, 18,000 cavalry and 53 heavy guns. Clive, for once, was daunted by the odds, but fortified the mango groves while he waited for the onslaught in a nearby hunting lodge.

The Battle

It came on 23 June and promised an easy victory for the Nawab. However, Mir Jafar had been left commanding the cavalry, even though he had already agreed with the British that his men would not fight. Other Nawab commanders were also bribed, as the British exploited the widespread dislike for the new ruler. Only the new army commander, Mir Madan, proved loyal with a strong following among the troops. However, when he began the battle with a determined attack on the British positions, a shot from one of Clive's cannon killed him. It was a major setback, as his closest followers went into immediate mourning and out of the fight.

Next came another monsoon downpour and Clive's soldiers took care to protect their weapons and keep their powder dry. The Nawab's men did not, however, and once the storm had passed, most of their weapons refused to fire. This was a catastrophe. The British bombardment scattered the Nawab's large body of infantry. Anxious to safeguard his small force, Clive held back until it was safe to send in his European infantry, the 39th Foot, which drove the Nawab's remaining infantry from the field.

The Outcome and Significance

For such a world-changing battle, casualties were light. Clearly, the double blow of their commander's death and the refusal of their weapons to fire, had broken the morale of the Nawab's men, but Clive's most decisive weapon had been bribes for the Nawab's officers to take no part in the battle. Siraj-ud-Daulah had many enemies and he was later captured by the forces of the new Nawab and executed. Mir Jafar later conspired with the Dutch against the British but their attack was defeated in November 1759. He was deposed and later reinstated, ruling until his death eight years later.

Bad weather, wet powder and fragile morale enabled a heavily outnumbered force to change the history of an entire subcontinent. Plassey provided no tactical lessons, except the value of professional attention to detail over apparently insuperable odds. It secured British rule in India for almost two centuries. Clive recognized the qualities of his Indian soldiers and established what would become the largest volunteer army in the world, with a vital role in both world wars.

A Siege Against the Odds

Where: Delhi, India
When: 1857
War: Indian Mutiny (1857–1858)
Combatants: British Government vs.
             Indian rebels
Casualties: British Government: 1,250;
             Indian rebels: 5,000

On 9 May 1857, rising discontent in India's Bengal Army boiled over into mutiny, when regiments at Meerut killed their British officers and civilians. The next day, they marched to Delhi to name the last Moghul Emperor, Bahadur Shah II, a pensioner of the British, as their leader (against his will). Significantly, a troop of one regiment, the 3rd Light Cavalry, remained loyal to the British throughout. With Delhi taken, the uprising spread rapidly. Rebels flocking to the city made it an essential target for the British. Since Bengal Army units were suspect, retaking the city would require troops from the Bombay and Madras armies, serving in the Punjab or on the Afghan Frontier and the first relieving force headed for Delhi a week later.

The Positions

The relieving force faced a daunting task. Delhi's stout walls and bastions bristled with artillery. The attackers set up camp on the Ridge, an 18-metre (60-foot) rock outcrop stretching down the western side of the city. Protected from the rear by a canal, it offered poor shelter from the heat or the monsoon and for weeks the attackers waited for reinforcements, while suffering constant rebel attacks from within the city. Gradually, more troops joined – mainly Sikhs, Gurkhas and Pathans of undoubted loyalty – and, finally, a siege train with 60 heavy guns and mortars to breach the city wall arrived on 6 September. On the next day the first battery began bombarding the city walls and bastions. But building more batteries depended on the devoted courage of Indian sappers working under heavy fire.

Above British engineers and Indian sappers under heavy fire as they lay mines under the Delhi fortifications in preparation for the attack on 14 September, which eventually took the city.

The Battle

Eventually ammunition ran short in the city and morale crumbled. On the night of 13 September the attackers prepared and before dawn the assault began. After blowing gunpowder charges laid by British and Indian sappers, three of the four columns were soon inside the city. Rebels attacked the fourth column, driving it back outside the Kabul Gate. Only when the guns of a nearby battery were turned on the rebels, followed by charges by British and Indian cavalry, was the attack resumed.

By this time, rebels had driven back attackers inside the city, with heavy casualties. For a time, withdrawal seemed the sensible option, but they held their positions and, after two days of savage house-to-house fighting, the British captured the rebel powder magazine on 16 September. Two days after that, Bahadur Shah and his family fled the city and Delhi was finally declared taken on September 21.

The Outcome and Significance

Crushing the rebellion across India lasted into 1858, as British and Indian troops hunted down rebels and supporters. After atrocities like the massacre of British women and children at Cawnpore, mercy was rare. Finally, order was restored and the Crown addressed many grievances that had created the mutiny. It also took over India's government from the East India Company. The mutiny would have succeeded had it not been for the majority of Indian soldiers remaining loyal and the Indian Army was radically reformed. After another 90 years of British rule, it was split into the present armies of India and Pakistan.

Normally, siege operations only take place where the attackers have a massive advantage in numbers and resources. Here, Delhi's importance as a centre of rebel resistance meant it had to be taken whatever the odds. To make this possible, rebels in other areas had to be disarmed and reinforcements summoned in large enough numbers. Until they arrived, the success of the battle depended on the attackers' ability to defend their siege operations against massive attacks from within the city.

Courage and Mobility

Where:	Isandlwana, Natal, South Africa
When:	1879
War:	Zulu War (1879)
Combatants:	Britain vs. Zululand
Casualties:	British: 1,330 killed;
	Zulus: 1,000 killed

Towards the end of the 19th century, Sir Bartle Frere, High Commissioner of Southern Africa, was intent on eliminating the threat he believed the Zulus presented to British rule in the area. He sent an unauthorized ultimatum to Cetshwayo, the Zulu ruler, on 11 December 1878. The harsh terms deliberately sought to provoke the Zulus to reject them. When they did, Frere sent Lord Chelmsford with an army into Zululand to extend British rule.

The Positions

Chelmsford believed the Zulus would avoid fighting troops armed with modern weapons, so he divided his army into five columns. He grouped two columns into his main advance and crossed the Buffalo River into Zululand on 11 January 1879. With 1,000 men of the 24th Foot, backed by Natal native troops, they crept slowly into Zulu territory, with supplies carried in cumbersome ox carts.

Unlike European armies, Zulu warriors were light and mobile and moved at ten times the speed of the invaders, covering 80 kilometres (50 miles) in half the time Chelmsford's army took to move just 16 kilometres (10 miles). Finally the British reached Isandlwana on 20 January, but neither dug defences nor even moved their wagons into a defensive circle, since no real threat was apparent.

The Battle

Persistent underestimation of Zulu fighting abilities had led Chelmsford to split his force. While he advanced with half his regulars to search for the Zulu army, it was the Zulus who found his camp at Isandlwana, defended by more than 1,000 men, a rocket troop and two seven-pounder guns. Cavalry scouts reported groups of Zulus approaching the camp on the morning of 23 January. A signal was sent to warn Chelmsford, as around 12,000 Zulus approached the camp in their classic buffalo-horn formation, with two extended wings running forward of the main body to envelop and surround their opponents in a Cannae manoeuvre (see page 13).

Colonel Pulleine ordered his British infantry out into a line to meet the Zulu attack and their brisk rifle fire imposed heavy casualties on warriors

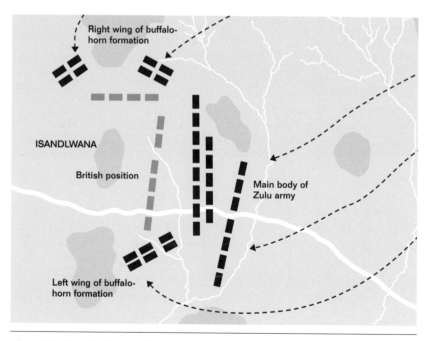

Above The Zulus' 'buffalo-horn' formation was instrumental in their victory as the two wings of the attack surrounded the British position.

armed with spears and flimsy shields. Nevertheless, the British position was already threatened, as warriors in the left horn of the formation began to outflank them. As the right wing of the British position ran short of ammunition, they had to fall back and eventually the entire force retreated into the camp. With no real defences, they were surrounded and completely overwhelmed by huge numbers of attackers, fighting hand-to-hand at odds of around ten to one. Groups were overwhelmed in turn, including one that had formed a square to resist attack. Finally the troops within the camp, and stragglers escaping down the river, were all cut down. (Civilians were spared on Cetshwayo's express orders). By 15.00 it was all over.

The Outcome and Significance

Isandlwana was Britain's worst colonial defeat and it ensured prompt retribution. Frere's policy of provoking the Zulus into war was given government backing for the first time and a reinforced army sent back into Zululand. They captured Cetshwayo, who had hoped throughout for a negotiated peace, and defeated his warriors in a series of engagements.

The defeat of British regulars by Zulu warriors in the Victorian heyday of empire remains a powerful example of the dangers resulting from underestimating an adversary. Belatedly, the British realized the Zulus' fighting qualities and the foolishness of adopting a line formation on open ground, even with regular troops. The Zulus' fast-moving tactics could easily outflank them, enabling their attackers to close in and use their stabbing and clubbing weapons. In all ensuing battles, the British treated them as the formidable adversaries they were, by forming defensive squares to repel their attacks (see page 68).

Defence Against Mass Attacks

Where: Rorke's Drift, Natal, South Africa
When: 1879
War: Zulu War (1879)
Combatants: Britain vs. Zululand
Casualties: British: 17; Zulus: 500

After a disastrous British defeat by the Zulus at Isandlwana in January 1879 (see page 65), Prince Dabulamanzi, younger brother of the Zulu ruler Cetshwayo, and his 4,000 soldiers were looking for targets of opportunity and a glorious victory of their own. They believed they had found it at Rorke's Drift, a former mission station and small military hospital on the Tugela river, garrisoned by a single company of the British 24th Foot and supporting troops, totalling 139 men – they faced truly terrifying odds.

The Positions

On 21 January, the defenders heard distant firing and scouts confirmed large numbers of approaching Zulus. They rushed to knock loopholes in the walls of the buildings for sharpshooters and built ramparts of mealie bags and cookie barrels for cover. However, before they could clear the approaches of undergrowth, the first 500 Zulus appeared, running headlong towards the station from the south.

The Battle

This first attack was hit by heavy fire. Nevertheless, the Zulus were able to close to 45 metres (147 feet) before veering around past the hospital wall to take cover in the uncleared undergrowth to the north-west. Soon they were joined by the remaining attackers who opened up heavy fire on the hospital. Finally they managed to set its thatched roof on fire and the British had to make frantic efforts to evacuate the wounded through the windows on the inside of the defences. Some died in the fire but the remaining soldiers expended all their ammunition keeping the Zulus out, using bayonets to continue the fight and earning three Victoria Crosses for their courage.

Zulu attacks shifted to the wall of biscuit barrels and mealie bags, which provided poor cover for the defenders. At dusk the British fell back to a smaller redoubt, which they had assembled beside the storehouse, for a last stand. Fierce attacks continued until midnight, with the oncoming Zulus suffering heavy casualties in the glare from the burning hospital. Nonetheless, the defenders were in an increasingly desperate situation when, at midnight, the pace of the attacks slackened.

The Zulus outside the perimeter went on firing until 04.00 when they withdrew out of sight. Three hours later, more Zulus appeared on the hills overlooking the mission. To the defenders' surprise and relief, no attacks resulted and finally the Zulus disappeared. The reason for their flight became clear with the approach of a relief column led by Lord Chelmsford. Rorke's Drift had held out against terrible odds, suffering 17 killed and 10 wounded, compared with an estimated 500 Zulus killed. Significantly, all the British dead had suffered bullet wounds rather than spear or knife wounds; the Zulus hadn't been able to get close enough to use their spears.

The Outcome and Significance

The defence won time for the British to recover their balance after the disaster of Isandlwana. Lord Chelmsford realized that the courage, ferocity and tactical skill of their opponents meant that they would need greater numbers to contain the threat they presented. In March 1879, the British defeated the Zulus at Khambula and, in April, they relieved a besieged British force at Eshowe. Finally, on 4 July 1879, British forces routed Cetshwayo's army at the battle of Ulundi.

Rorke's Drift demonstrated that a company of regular soldiers with modern weapons and improvised fortifications could successfully defeat 30 times their number of brave and determined warriors. It showed the huge advantages of modern weaponry and training to a small but professional British Army. The soldiers also had the huge added bonus of defence in depth, with a position made as secure as possible from meagre resources, and the option of falling back to keep their attackers at bay and under continuing fire.

Part Four:
World Wars

Speed Defeats Two Armies

Where: Tannenberg, East Prussia, Germany
When: 1914
War: First World War (1914–1918)
Combatants: Germany vs. Russia
Casualties: Germans: 12,000; Russians: 50,000

In August 1914, the Germans faced the Russians on their Eastern Front. Since the enemy outnumbered their own armies on both fronts put together, the Germans needed a speedy victory to deflect the threat. However, within weeks, two Russian armies advanced into German territory. The First Army approached Königsberg in East Prussia. As the German Eighth Army rushed to defend the city, the Russian Second Army, further south, was outflanking the Masurian Lakes to attack the Germans from behind. However, because the Russians had outrun landlines and lacked trained cryptographers, they radioed orders in plain language, which told the Germans their intentions.

The Positions

German units advanced toward Königsberg but then fell back to the River Vistula to avoid the Russians' outflanking movement, delayed owing to transport problems. However, they were still outnumbered almost two to one, and faced losing East Prussia. Already the Königsberg defences were only manned on the eastern sectors to face the Russian First Army, while remaining German units were rushed more than 160 kilometres (100 miles) south-west to face the Russian Second Army near Tannenberg.

The Battle

At first, the Second Army pushed the Germans back, until the XX Corps dug in to stop the advance. The Russians then pushed forward on either side of the German positions. The German XVII Corps, rushed forward by train, was in time to stop the larger thrust to the north-east. Meanwhile, local radio intercepts around Königsberg showed the Russian First Army was still not moving to join the Second Army in crushing the Germans at Tannenberg.

The battle against the Russian Second Army opened on 26 August 1914 with a furious German counterattack on the right Russian pincer, pushing it into headlong retreat. While the German XX Corps still held, the XVII Corps began pounding the Russian left pincer with heavy artillery, forcing this, too, to pull back. Only the Russian centre was holding, until ordered to break through the German lines at Tannenberg. Owing to continuing supply problems, this too failed – Russian railroads had tracks laid to a broader gauge than German, causing huge transport delays. On 28 August, they began a retreat to the Russian border but the advancing Germans cut off the Russian centre to the east of Tannenberg and pounded it with heavy artillery.

At long last the Russian First Army, still confronting Königsberg, sent a relieving force. Harried by German cavalry, this failed to reach the Second Army and by 30 August, the fighting was over. The Russians suffered 50,000 casualties, with some 95,000 taken prisoner, against German casualties of about 12,000. The Germans captured more than 500 guns and 60 trainloads of captured equipment.

The Outcome and Significance

The Russian First Army soon retreated back across the border and never again threatened German territory. However, worried at possibly losing East Prussia, the German General Staff withdrew an entire army from the Western Front and sent it eastwards. Though both late and unnecessary, it seems likely that the loss of those forces in the West meant the German advance was halted before Paris, resulting in four years of bloody trench warfare and final defeat.

Tannenberg showed the value of operating on home ground with interior lines of supply and communication against two separate threats. The Germans' speed of manoeuvre enabled them to defeat two larger Russian armies in turn; because the Germans could switch their army quickly to tackle one enemy army in isolation, they could defeat this before turning back to attack the second and drive it back on to its own ground.

Failed Landings Prepare for D-Day

Where: Gallipoli peninsula, Turkey
When: 1915
War: First World War (1914–1918)
Combatants: Allies vs. Turkey
Casualties: Allies: 140,000; Turkish: 196,000

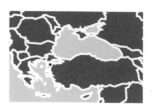

In 1915, the Allies planned to create a supply route to the Russian front through the Dardanelles, stretching from the Mediterranean into the Black Sea. When Turkish shore batteries beat back Allied warships in March, the Allies decided to land troops on the Gallipoli peninsula instead. After six weeks' delay, on 25 April, British and French troops landed, reinforced by their empires' soldiers. Their opponents, in the meantime, had strengthened the peninsula's defences.

The Positions

The Turks stationed two divisions on the eastern face of the peninsula, another two on the western shore at the base of the peninsula and two more at its southern tip. In fact, the two main landing sites were the beaches around Cape Helles at the tip of the peninsula and on the western shore at a bay, later known as Anzac Cove, where the Australians and New Zealanders landed.

The Battle

In both cases, the attackers landed successfully but suffered heavy casualties later on. However, the Turks failed to force them back into the sea, creating a pattern for the following months. Each side delivered attack after attack for trivial gains and huge casualties, and then brought in reinforcements. The Allies increased from five divisions to 16, while the Turks increased their strength to 15 divisions, giving neither side a decisive enough advantage for victory.

The result was a battle of attrition, made worse by problems of heat, flies, mosquitoes and dysentery. When Allied troops threatened to take the high ground and link up their positions, the Turks were able to rush in reinforcements and limit the damage caused. The last Allied attack was made on Hill 60 on 29 August 1915 and when the Turks beat them back, the campaign was all but over. Evacuating under Turkish fire now threatened a virtual massacre.

The Outcome and Significance

Ironically, one objective of the campaign had been to deter other nations from joining the Turkish-German alliance. Its failure resulted in Bulgaria joining the enemy in the autumn, offering a land route for Germany to send heavy siege guns to crush the Allied positions into submission. Evacuation became pressing, therefore. After predictions of up to 50 per cent casualties, careful preparations were made to prevent the Turks learning of their opponents' intention to pull out.

By now, men were dying from exposure in heavy snowstorms. Troops began leaving on 7 December 1915, with the last Anzacs departing 12 days later. The rear guard remained quiet to tempt Turkish attacks and then put up heavy fire to stop them, realizing that their numbers were dwindling. In addition, ruses like timer devices to actuate self-firing rifles deceived the Turks, until they belatedly realized what was afoot, and launched a final attack on the British on 6 January 1916. This was repulsed and the last troops left three days later. Not a single man was lost in the evacuation. The campaign was celebrated as a Turkish triumph, in spite of 196,000 casualties, almost 40 per cent greater than Allied losses. Surging morale enabled them to defeat a British force in Iraq and push into the Sinai Peninsula before stronger Allied forces turned the tables and finally defeated them.

Gallipoli squandered the value of surprise. The overambitious campaign to force the passage of the Dardanelles decayed into an unwinnable and costly land campaign. If seaborne landings are to succeed, the invaders have to reinforce their bridgehead more quickly from the sea than the defenders can do by land. At Gallipoli, delays in assembling the forces and carrying out the landings allowed the Turks to create unassailable defences. Learning this terrible lesson ensured the success of the D-Day landings of 1944, following massive deceptions and a rapid build-up of troops within the bridgehead.

Strategy of Attrition

Where: Verdun and the Somme, France
When: 1916
War: First World War (1914–1918)
Combatants: Allies vs. Germany
Casualties: (Verdun) French: 163,000;
             Germans: 143,000;
             (Somme) British: 420,000;
             French: 200,000; Germans: 329,000

Defenders, well dug in and equipped with machine guns, imposed a bloody stalemate for almost four years on the First World War's Western Front. In early 1916, the Germans attacked the city and fortress chain of Verdun, a target the French would be forced to defend at heavy cost, at the risk of defeat. The battle was one of the longest and bloodiest of all time, while the British disaster on the Somme resulted from the need to relieve pressure on Verdun. Time after time, attackers were cut down in No Man's Land between the trenches.

The Positions
Verdun was ringed by 18 massive forts over a 8-kilometre (5-mile) zone. However, many had been stripped of weapons to meet the needs of other sectors, while the Germans outnumbered the French almost two to one, with better communications and shorter supply lines.

The Battle
The Germans attacked on 21 February 1916 with a 10-hour bombardment by 1,200 guns on a 40-kilometre (25-mile) front. Storm troops with grenades and flamethrowers cleared the French trenches and on 25 February they captured Fort Douaumont, keystone of the French defences. The French were rushing men and supplies down the 'Voie Sacrée', the narrow road to Verdun, swept by German fire. However, the Germans were now advancing beyond their own artillery and into the sights of French gunners, who stopped their

Above French gunners keep watch from the observation post of a carefully screened trench at Verdun.

main attack with heavy casualties. A failed assault on Fort Souville on 21 June proved the high point of the German offensive.

French appeals for a British attack on the Somme, to lift pressure on Verdun, produced the huge offensive of 1 July 1916. Unfortunately, security was poor, and the Germans knew what was coming from the preliminary artillery bombardment. When the eight-day barrage lifted, German machine gunners emerged from deep dugouts to mow down the first attackers. During that first day, almost 20,000 British troops were killed with twice that number wounded and gains were measured in yards. In places, 10 days' terrible fighting was needed to reach the main German trench line but the Germans were already transferring troops from Verdun to plug the defences. The French wanted continuing British pressure to prevent the Germans releasing reinforcements back to Verdun. Finally, on 21 October 1916, they began their own Verdun offensive. After three days of blasting with one-ton (1,000 kg) shells from 16-inch (40.5-cm) railroad guns, the French recaptured Fort Douaumont, and the Germans eventually withdrew on 2 November. French pressure finally forced the Germans back to their starting positions where, on 19 December, they finally admitted defeat.

On the Somme, when the last attack petered out in heavy snowstorms on 18 November, total British gains amounted to 11 kilometres (7 miles) for 420,000 casualties, with 200,000 French losses and half a million Germans. These exceeded Verdun's figures of 377,000 French casualties against 329,000 Germans. The firing of 36 million French and German shells had obliterated another 100,000 men and human bones are still found regularly after more than 80 years.

The Outcome and Significance

Later analysis showed that the halting of the first German Verdun offensive resulted from British and French pressure on the Somme in summer 1916. Furthermore, their final Verdun defeat was aided by their having transferred 42 divisions to hold the Somme defences, leaving their entire army with one single reserve division.

After the prolonged and bloody stalemate of the First World War, the French decided that even stronger defences were needed to protect them against another Verdun, and built the huge fortress chain of the Maginot Line along France's borders with Germany and Italy. The Germans, on the other hand, adopted fast-moving mobile warfare, producing the breakthrough of May 1940, where they outflanked the Maginot Line without it obstructing them at all.

Ending Stalemate

Where: Amiens, northern France
When: 1918
War: First World War (1914–1918)
Combatants: Allies vs. Germany
Casualties: Allies: 22,000; Germans: 74,000

March 1918 saw the end of the First World War's trench-bound deadlock. Desperate German attacks, using troops switched from the Eastern Front after Russia's capitulation, failed to defeat the Allies before American reinforcements arrived. After large initial gains, a resolute Allied defence halted their advance in its tracks and they began retreating on 20 July. The Australians had held the vital rail junction of Amiens in northern France and this was set to be the site of a massive Allied offensive in August 1918. Three new Allied weapons came into play: large numbers of tanks, much more accurate artillery fire and surprise. Previously, guns needed a long series of ranging shots to correct their aim, showing the enemy an attack was coming. New aerial photos enabled troops to aim guns without firing, so a barrage opened as an attack began, in complete surprise.

The Positions

The Germans knew that the presence of the Canadian Infantry Corps would indicate a planned attack, so the Allies mounted a careful deception to suggest they were being sent north instead. Two Canadian infantry battalions, a radio transmitter and a casualty clearing station were sent to Ypres, suggesting the rest were due to follow. To further avoid drawing attention to the Amiens sector in particular, the British moved more than 500 tanks and almost 1,400 guns and howitzers at night, along roads covered in straw to deaden noise, and masked by the noise of air patrols flying along the entire front. By morning they had hidden their new troops and weapons in carefully camouflaged positions.

This convinced the Germans that the British would attack east of Rheims or further north in Flanders. They themselves had six divisions in the trench lines in front of Amiens, with two facing the adjacent French First Army on the right and another two in reserve. In fact, the Allies had massed three British divisions north of the Somme, with five Australian divisions south of the river, four Canadian divisions on their right and 12 French divisions to the south, providing an encouraging and unsuspected superiority.

The Battle

At 04.20 on 8 August 1918, the Allies opened the battle without warning, with a fierce artillery bombardment out of a thick blanket of mist. At the same time, the leading troops left their trenches and moved quickly across No Man's Land, less than 450 metres (1,476 feet) wide along this stretch and out of sight of the German machine gunners. So complete was the surprise that German gunners only began replying after five minutes. Their first shells fell on the now empty Allied positions, as the leading troops advanced behind an accurate creeping barrage just 55 metres (180 feet) in front.

Three hours after the attack began, the Germans had fallen back more than 3 kilometres (2 miles). By 11.00, the leading Canadian and Australian troops had captured a German divisional staff sitting down to breakfast, confident they were still far behind the lines. As the advance continued, Allied fighters machine-gunned German reserves, while tanks, armoured cars, and even cavalry poured through the gap in their defences. By the end of the first day, the Allies had pushed more than 11 kilometres (7 miles) into the German lines and torn open a 24-kilometre (15-mile) wide breach.

Some problems still remained, however. Tanks proved so unreliable that most were out of action through breakdown by the end of the day. Though the Germans managed to bridge the gap in their defences, they lost 30,000 killed, wounded and prisoners, against 8,800 Allied casualties on what the Chief of their General Staff called 'the black day of the German Army' and the most decisive Allied victory of the war.

The Outcome and Significance

German morale plummeted and more and more troops began to surrender. Jammed roads and poor communications held up the advancing Allies more than enemy action but two days later a general German retreat began. Over

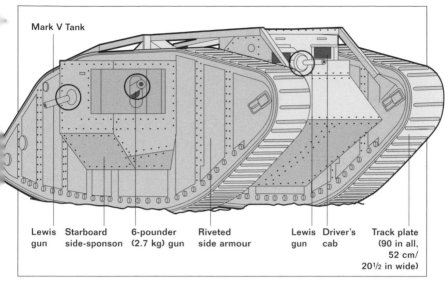

Mark V Tank

| Lewis gun | Starboard side-sponson | 6-pounder (2.7 kg) gun | Riveted side armour | Lewis gun | Driver's cab | Track plate (90 in all, 52 cm/ 20½ in wide) |

Above The Mark V tank was the first to be used effectively in warfare; it played a key role in ending the stalemate of the western front and added a new element to the mobility of forces.

five days, British troops advanced 19 kilometres (12 miles), and by 27 August the Germans had lost 50,000 prisoners and more than 500 guns. The offensive continued for the remaining three months of the war. It proved the Germans had been defeated on the battlefield, despite later Nazi claims that defeatist politicians had stabbed them in the back.

Both sides learned different lessons from the battle. For the Allies, Amiens demonstrated the value of deception and surprise in ensuring the success of an attack, even against strong defences. For the Germans, their crushing defeat spurred them to develop the combination of movement and firepower that had brought their successes earlier in 1918, adding tanks to produce the powerful concept of blitzkrieg that won so many early victories in the Second World War.

Blitzkrieg Breakthrough

Where: Ardennes, France
When: 1940
War: Second World War (1939–1945)
Combatants: Allies vs. Germany
Casualties: Allies: 360,000; Germans: 155,000

Restricted to a small army by the Versailles Treaty (1918), Germany built small elite formations of tanks and motorized infantry to break through enemy defences, in a mechanized version of the infiltration tactics of their last offensives during the First World War. They would bypass stubborn enemy positions, leaving the second-line infantry to deal with them. If this failed, dive-bombers, called in by ground commanders, would replace cumbersome heavy artillery. The whole doctrine was known as *Blitzkrieg* or 'lightning warfare' for its combination of power and speed.

The Positions

After conquering Poland, the Germans faced the French and British on the Western Front. Numbers were almost equal, including the initially neutral Dutch and Belgians, but French tanks were placed in small groups along the entire front, rather than massed in armoured divisions like those of the Germans. Furthermore, most French troops were based on the German frontier in the static fortifications of the Maginot Line.

The British Army, barred from neutral Belgium, waited on the border, ready to cross only when the enemy attacked. The Germans realized there was one clear weakness in the Allied defences: the narrow roads and dense forests of the Ardennes, thought to be impassable and known to be lightly defended. Here they made their breakthrough.

The Battle

The blow fell on 10 May 1940, with heavy attacks on Holland and Belgium. This triggered a British advance into Belgium to face the Germans, unaware of the armoured units hidden from aerial reconnaissance in the Ardennes.

That same evening, German panzers and their supporting troops emerged from hiding, ahead of French units rushing to meet them, and in three days their spearheads reached the French defences on the River Meuse. After four hours of dive-bombing the French on the opposite bank, the Germans crossed at four places at 16.00. One attack was repelled, but the others succeeded and, by 18.00, they were ferrying their tanks, guns and troops across the river.

It was the start of a flood. By the following day, the panzers were almost 32 kilometres (20 miles) into the vulnerable rear areas. Two days later, they were 64 kilometres (40 miles) behind the front, and on 21 May they reached the English Channel, cutting off the British and French in the north from the rest of the country. The huge French reserves sitting in the Maginot Line fortresses had hardly fired a shot but behind them their country was crumbling. By the end of May, the British had retreated to the port of Dunkirk, where more than 330,000 men were safely evacuated to England, though without their heavy weapons and equipment. Barely six weeks after the initial invasion, blitzkrieg had

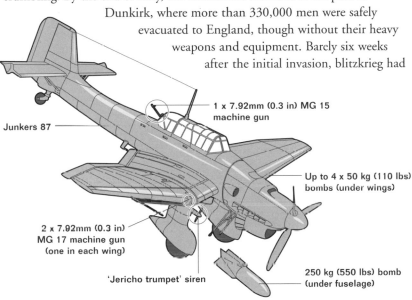

1 x 7.92mm (0.3 in) MG 15 machine gun

Junkers 87

Up to 4 x 50 kg (110 lbs) bombs (under wings)

2 x 7.92mm (0.3 in) MG 17 machine gun (one in each wing)

'Jericho trumpet' siren

250 kg (550 lbs) bomb (under fuselage)

Above Air support, including the accurate attacks by Junkers 87 'Stuka' dive bombers, aided the advance of ground forces during the blitzkrieg attacks.

effectively beaten Europe's premier military power and the French agreed to an armistice on 25 June. German casualties amounted to a total of 156,000 killed and wounded, a trivial cost by the standards of the previous war.

For the British, there was a small ray of hope. A counterattack with heavily armoured Matilda tanks heading south from Arras into the right flank of the German advance had given General Rommel, commanding Seventh Panzer Division, a severe shock. Fortunately for him, panzer divisions were equipped with mobile 88-mm (3½ in) anti-aircraft guns to defend against Allied aircraft. Here he put them to use as anti-tank guns, to beat off the British tanks. Later in the war, in its anti-tank role, the '88' earned a fearsome reputation, as its shells could pierce thick armour with ease.

The Outcome and Significance

The sharpest blow was the loss of a British foothold on the European mainland. Regaining that foothold would take the massive D-Day landings on the Normandy beaches four years later, followed by months of bitter fighting to take what the Germans had seized so easily in 1940.

Determined to avoid repeating the First World War trench-warfare deadlock, the Germans used the speed and reliability of modern tanks to revive mobile warfare. Blitzkrieg was a most powerful concept and countering it took time and experience. However, it could only triumph in the right conditions. On the Russian front, German panzer forces could cover huge distances at high speed in favourable weather; they encircled and crushed entire Russian armies in the opening weeks of the 1941 campaign. The same effectiveness was shown by General Patton's American armour charging through France in the Normandy breakout of 1944 as quickly as the Germans had done in 1940. But roads blocked by mud, snow or shellfire caused crippling delays, and specialized anti-tank guns and handheld weapons, like bazookas and rocket-propelled grenades, enabled defenders to hit back. Finally, under total enemy air superiority, tanks could barely move without attack, as the Germans in Normandy and the Iraqis in the first Gulf War found to their cost.

Cutting off a Retreat

Where: Beda Fomm, North Africa
When: 1941
War: Second World War (1939–1945)
Combatants: Britain vs. Italy
Casualties: British: 500; Italians: 3,000

In late 1940, the Italian 10th Army invaded Egypt. Advancing slowly, it halted at Sidi Barrani to wait for supplies. A smaller British force attacked on 8 December 1940 and more and more Italian positions began to fall. In February 1941, the entire Italian army began to pull back west towards Libya and safety, whereupon a small and fast-moving British force was sent on a short cut across the desert to block the Italians' coastal escape route.

The Positions

Just 2,000 men with armoured cars, a battery of 25-pounder (11 kg) cannon and another of 37-mm (1½ in) anti-tank guns, finally completed their 240-kilometre (150-mile) dash on 5 February 1941, ahead of their cruiser tanks. Steering by compass, the armoured cars cut the coast road at a small hamlet and mosque called Beda Fomm, with no sign of the Italians. They had won their race by the narrowest of margins. As they dug in to block the road, mines were laid and just two hours later, dust clouds to the north warned of the approaching Italian army. Soon the British would face odds of 60 to 1.

The Battle

The Italians suffered total surprise. A leading vehicle set off a mine and British shells burst among them. But as more Italian units arrived, the pressure on the British increased. Fortunately for the blockaders, the next to arrive were the British cruiser tanks, which reached the coast road further north, opposite a line of Italian trucks, which they set on fire. Finally, Royal Engineers laid more mines in the gathering darkness to bolster British defences.

Fighting began again on the cold, rainy morning of 6 February. At a small hill called the Pimple, 19 British tanks faced 60 Italian – firing from cover, they knocked out many Italians, but still more came. Italian artillery battered the British defences, and by 15.00, they were on the point of breakthrough. Then another group of British tanks arrived out of the desert and drove the Italians back to their starting point, before settling down for a second uneasy night.

The next morning, the remaining 30 Italian tanks made one last attack. One by one they knocked out the British anti-tank guns, though taking heavy casualties. The attack finally stalled when the last British anti-tank gun, crewed by the battery commander, his orderly and a battery cook, knocked out the last Italian tank. The Italian infantry tried a final bayonet charge, which petered out when their commander fell. By 21.00 the fighting was over and the Italians surrendered.

The Outcome and Significance

It was a staggering victory. The Italian 10th Army lost 3,000 killed and no less than 130,000 taken prisoner, with around 400 tanks and 1,300 guns, against British losses of just under 500 killed and 1,200 wounded. It seemed victory in North Africa was assured. Yet within weeks the German invasion of Greece forced units to be sent to meet this new threat. The suddenly depleted remainder had to pause where they were, while Hitler rushed to the aid of his ally. Within weeks the first of Rommel's Afrika Korps were disembarking at the port of Tripoli and a much more hard-fought North African campaign would last two more years before final Allied victory.

Beda Fomm showed how a determined attack by a small and fast-moving force could intercept and defeat a much larger retreating army. In the end, the collapse in Italian morale that followed the cutting of their line of retreat proved decisive, where a more resolute force might have broken through to escape.

Japanese Back-door Invasion

Where:	Malaya Peninsula, Singapore
When:	1942
War:	Second World War (1939–1945)
Combatants:	Britain vs. Japan
Casualties:	British: 7,000; Japanese: 4,400

During the Second World War, Singapore was designed to repel seaborne assaults, relying on the protection of the Malayan jungles on its landward side. However, the British grossly underestimated the enemy's ability and never contemplated a real attack. Yet in four days of fighting, Japanese air attacks virtually eliminated local RAF squadrons and sank two British battleships. On the ground, their troops moved with Napoleonic speed and mobility, outflanking the British, Australian and Indian troops sent to stop them.

The Positions

The Japanese let nothing hold them up, bypassing opposition and infiltrating enemy lines using jungle tracks. On 11 January, the Malayan capital, Kuala Lumpur, fell and on 31 January the last defending troops withdrew across the causeway to the island of Singapore itself. Here the British had 85,000 men to defend the

Right One of Singapore's 38-cm (15-inch) coastal defence guns, which were supplied only with armour-piercing shells instead of the more effective high-explosive shells.

city against 35,000 trained and battle-hardened Japanese. The British commander, Lieutenant General Arthur Percival, overestimated enemy strength, and spread out his units across the entire 96-kilometre (70-mile) width of the island, grossly overstretching his forces.

The Battle

The Allies won a week's respite by blowing up the causeway. Meanwhile, the Japanese shelled all the airfields except one, denying them to RAF aircraft. Finally on 9 February, the first 4,000 troops were carried across the Johore Strait by landing craft to hit the north-western sector defended by the Australians. Infiltrating through creeks and waterways that split the defenders' positions, the Japanese pushed them back. Through the day, heavy air battles eliminated most surviving RAF fighters and they evacuated the remainder.

More Japanese landings were made on 10 February to the north and in the south-west. Difficulties in communications led to defenders on the western side pulling back to avoid encirclement, which allowed the Japanese to land amphibious tanks on the original landing beach and force their way towards the centre of the city. Fighting continued until 14 February. By the following morning, ammunition was running short, but the Japanese supply position was just as critical. Their commander bluffed with a demand for an immediate Allied surrender, which was agreed at 05.15.

The Outcome and Significance

The loss of Singapore was one of the worst British defeats to its Eastern Empire, with around 100,000 personnel taken prisoner. The Japanese went on to capture the Philippines and the Dutch East Indies, and their advance was only stopped in the north of Burma and astride the border with India.

The British lost Singapore largely owing to its inadequacy as a defensive position. Instead of the planned naval forces arriving as soon as fighting broke out, demands of the war in the West meant naval and air reinforcements never arrived. Even existing defences were poor: Singapore's massive naval defence guns were limited to armour-piercing shells, designed for use against enemy warships, but useless against enemy troops, when high-explosive shells would have been much more effective.

A Return to Trench Warfare

Where: El Alamein, North Africa
When: 1942
War: Second World War (1939–1945)
Combatants: Britain vs. Germany and Italy
Casualties: British: approximately 27,000;
              Germans and Italians:
              approximately 47,000

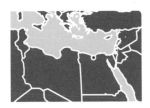

In the final stage of the North African campaign, the Allies halted Rommel's Afrika Korps at a bottleneck near the small railroad halt of El Alamein. Here, a narrow gap between the sea and the salt marshes of the Qattara Depression provided a strong defensive position. But before they could counterattack, they had to defeat Rommel's final attempt to break through their own defences. Key to the whole position was the Alam Halfa ridge, crammed with British anti-tank guns and protected by sand too soft for tanks. To prevent Rommel outflanking the ridge on firmer sand, the British left forged maps on the battlefield showing the ridge as undefended and the sand as hard enough for tanks. Lacking accurate maps of his own, Rommel took the bait and attacked the ridge on the night of 30 August 1942. The British drove him back after three days of hard fighting and heavy losses. Their moment had come.

The Positions

The strength of the El Alamein position meant it was as difficult for the British to break through to the west as it was for Rommel to head for Cairo. Surprise would be vital, but deception difficult in the desert's pitiless clarity. Montgomery planned to attack in the north, so the British brought in huge forces of dummy tanks, guns and supplies in the south. In addition, a dummy water pipeline was under construction, heading for the southern end of the line, at a rate suggesting that an attack could not come before the end of the year. Meanwhile, Montgomery brought in the real units for the coming battle at night, placing them in carefully camouflaged positions, hidden from German eyes.

The Battle

Fighting began on 23 October, with Allied attacks in the southern sector reinforcing the deception. Meanwhile, in the north, troops with mine detectors strove in darkness to clear tank paths through German minefields 8 kilometres (5 miles) wide, so the British armour could break through and meet Rommel's panzers head on. Unfortunately the minefields were much wider than expected and dust stirred up by the tanks added to the confusion. When dawn came, the armour was still held up in the minefields and what should have been a decisive attack became a battle of attrition between opposing tanks and infantry.

For days on end, the fighting swayed back and forth across the lines, as the British brought more forces up from the south to reinforce the northern

Left Bernard Montgomery, commander of the British Eighth Army in North Africa in 1942.

attacks, but there was still no breakthrough. Rommel himself, lulled by the deception campaign into taking sick leave in Germany, returned to the front on 26 October. Realizing that the north was the decisive sector, he ordered all his armoured forces to meet the threat.

This proved fatal. By now Allied aircraft and submarines had sunk so many tankers that the Afrika Korps was desperately short of fuel. German tanks sent north could not move back when stopped by British tanks and had to remain in the open, where Allied aircraft knocked them out. Fighting continued up and down the front until the British broke through the German minefields on 1 November. Their advancing tanks ran straight into one of Rommel's favourite defences – a hidden screen of formidable 88-mm anti-tank guns. Losses mounted, but at the end British reinforcements were able to break through. With almost no tanks left, the Germans had no option but to retreat.

The Outcome and Significance

On 4 November, with trapped units being forced to surrender, Rommel disobeyed Hitler's orders to stand fast. He began a retreat, with the British snapping at his heels, all the way to Tunisia. Though El Alamein had been a vital Allied victory, Rommel managed to take the bulk of his army with him, to take refuge in the French fortifications of the Mareth Line along the southern border of Tunisia. Though much tough fighting lay ahead, by May 1943 the last German forces in North Africa surrendered and the long campaign was over.

El Alamein was, essentially, a First World War battle with trench lines, barbed wire and minefields giving the advantage to the defence. Overturning that balance in favour of the attackers meant careful preparation, a clever and ambitious deception plan, a huge advantage in numbers and weapons and a long and gruelling battle to break through into open country behind the lines, aided by air superiority. In almost all respects, it was a vital rehearsal for the D-Day landings and breakout battles of 1944 (see page 99).

Defeating Blitzkrieg

Where: Kursk, Russia
When: 1943
War: Second World War (1939–1945)
Combatants: Germany vs. Russia
Casualties: Germans: 50,000;
             Russians: 180,000

The attack on the Kursk salient – a massive bulge into the centre of the German defences – was planned as the ultimate blitzkrieg attack. Yet Russian spies inside Germany warned their masters of the impending assault and two months of German postponements gave the Russians time to build up huge defences of their own. When the attack finally began, on 5 July 1943, the Russians had fortified Kursk way beyond German expectations.

The Positions

Two German forces would attack from the northern and southern flanks of the 180-kilometre wide, 140-kilometre deep (120 by 90 miles) salient between Orel in the north and Kharkov in the south, to produce their usual Cannae encirclement (see page 12). These attacks involved 50 divisions – one-third of them armoured – and some 750,000 men. Both northern and southern pincers were to meet near Kursk before turning east and advancing as far as the Don River. In reply, the Russians laid a million land mines, dug 4,800 kilometres (3,000 miles) of trenches and packed the whole area with troops and weapons: roughly one-quarter of the entire Red Army's manpower and artillery, one-third of its air force and almost half its tank forces. Instead of the superiority in numbers usually needed for a successful attack, the Germans faced heavy odds from the start.

The Battle

Heavy artillery barrages and air attacks opened the fighting on 5 July. The Russians managed to knock out half the German batteries and their air force made a huge preemptive strike to foil the usual German tactic of bombing

Russian airfields before an offensive. Nevertheless, the Luftwaffe inflicted huge Russian losses, although the latter fared better the next day. Meanwhile, panzer losses were also heavy. Tanks and assault guns broke down in Russian minefields, sitting targets for Russian guns and aircraft. On the northern front, the Germans failed to concentrate their tanks, and much of the fighting depended on the infantry. Initially advancing on a 40-kilometre (25-mile) front, progress slowed and narrowed until the attack stalled on 10 July, 16 kilometres (10 miles) into the multilayered Russian defences.

The southern attack had more of the German tank strength and progress was faster, with fewer losses. But Russian tactics of grouping anti-tank guns to fire on individual targets proved highly effective. Even so, continuing German advances forced the Russians to send in their reserves to stem the attack. The crisis came on 12 July, when the Germans concentrated their entire southern tank reserves to punch a final gap through the Russian lines. Only by rushing the Fifth Guards Tank Army into the gap at Prokhorovka, were the Russians able to halt the attack after eight hours' fighting and massive losses.

The Outcome and Significance

The German losses of 50,000 at Kursk were infinitely more damaging than the 180,000 suffered by their opponents. The Red Army remained strong enough to launch a huge attack to the north of the Kursk salient on 12 July, threatening two more German armies with encirclement. The Luftwaffe knocked out huge numbers of advancing Russian tanks, using dive-bombers armed with 30-mm (1-in) cannon capable of punching through Soviet armour, and eventually the attack was beaten off. However, this new threat forced the final withdrawal of the Germans from the Kursk battlefield.

The German attempt to eliminate the Kursk salient, to shorten their Eastern Front defences, created the greatest armoured battle of all time. Kursk was the first time multilayered defences had stopped a massive armoured attack and was successful against conditions that would otherwise have been ideal for blitzkrieg. By stopping the German advance, the Russians could then launch their own, more successful, offensive further north. The Russians continued to hold the initiative until the end of the war.

Countering Mobile Forces

Where:	Stalingrad, Russia
When:	1942–43
War:	Second World War (1939–1945)
Combatants:	Germany vs. Russia
Casualties:	Germans: approx. 750,000;
	Russians: approx. one million

In summer 1942, the Germans advanced into southern Russia, towards the Caucusus oilfields and the industrial city of Stalingrad on the Volga. The oil was deferred for the coup of seizing the city named for the Soviet dictator. As a result, the Germans' advantage in fast and mobile warfare gave way to bloody street fighting which suited Russian strengths.

The Positions

By September, the German Sixth Army had pushed the Russians back to four small bridgeheads on the bank of the Volga in bitter fighting – one main railway station changed hands 14 times in six hours. As more units were dragged in, the vulnerable German flanks, stretching back 64 kilometres (40 miles) to the Don River, were left to grossly overstretched Italian, Hungarian and Romanian units. During the bitter weather of November, the Russians secretly massed three armies north of this German salient, with two more on the southern side.

The Battle

The Russians attacked the northern German flank on 19 November 1942, and the southern flank a day later. The defenders fought bravely, but ran out of ammunition and Russian units pushed on into the Sixth Army rear areas. On 22 November, the northern and southern Russian pincers closed at Kalach, 64 kilometres (40 miles) west of Stalingrad and almost 300,000

Opposite Red Army soldiers amongst ruins of a house during the street fighting of the Battle of Stalingrad, 1942.

German soldiers were cut off. This was not yet hopeless, as German units had been encircled before and usually broke out successfully. But the numbers were greater and the supply situation much worse. The Sixth Army had sent most of its stores and transport to the rear as unnecessary in street fighting. The Luftwaffe tried to resupply by air but even under favourable conditions only one-eighth of the army's daily needs could be met, and worsening weather and increasing Russian air attacks made even this impossible.

The Fourth Panzer Army tried, from 12 December, to batter a way through the Russian lines but progress was slow and the Stalingrad units lacked enough food, fuel, ammunition, and vehicles to fight to meet them. Even this faint hope faded when, on 16 December, more Russian forces attacked the Don front line, pushing it back 240 kilometres (150 miles) and creating another massive encirclement. The trapped army now had no chance.

Russian pressure began to crush the pocket, and in an ironic reversal of fate, the Germans had to defend the city ruins. By 25 January, the Russians had captured the airfields used for supplies and for evacuating wounded. Russian terms were ignored on Hitler's orders, but on the last day of January they forced the German commander, Field Marshal von Paulus, to surrender on capturing his headquarters in the ruined GUM department store. The rest of the survivors, numbering 91,000, surrendered on 2 February.

The Outcome and Significance

The battle was a disaster for the German Army and the human cost had a devastating effect on morale at home. Those captured faced a decade in Russian prison camps and only 5,000 survived to return to Germany in 1955. Russian casualties totalled more than a million in the Stalingrad battles.

The German Army in Russia had won its victories through mobility and speed but in Stalingrad it was wasted in city fighting, and left itself vulnerable to a massive Russian counterstroke. The Battle of Stalingrad underlined two harsh military lessons: not to waste the speed and shock effect of tanks in street fighting and not to overstretch flanks in attacking a distant objective.

Honing Air Bombardment

Where: Tarawa Atoll, Gilbert Islands,
               Central Pacific
When: 1943
War: Second World War (1939–45)
Combatants: America vs. Japan
Casualties: Americans: 1,600; Japanese: 5,000

American strategy against Japan involved building airfields on remote island bases to allow the bombing of Japan itself. As US strength grew, the Japanese resolved to make their enemy pay more dearly for each capture. For the Americans to take the Mariana Islands, within bombing range of Japan, they first needed bases on the Marshall Islands, northeast of Guadalcanal and before that they needed to clear their seaborne communications by capturing the base of Tarawa Atoll in the Gilbert Islands. Previously, they had attacked islands large enough to hide their intentions and land troops before the enemy could react. But in future operations on these smaller islands, concealment was impossible and costly frontal attacks essential.

The Positions

Tarawa was one of the most heavily fortified bases in the Pacific. Five thousand Japanese defenders built concrete barriers under water and laid mines offshore to force landing craft into zones swept by artillery. They built machine-gun posts, deep underground blockhouses and defence posts of coconut logs and coral, carefully camouflaged for maximum surprise and proof against heavy bombardment. To take the island, the US Navy brought up seven battleships and seven heavy cruisers for the initial bombardment, supported by 34 destroyers and eight carriers.

The Battle

The naval bombardment began on 20 November 1943, and lasted for half an hour before halting for a carrier dive-bomber strike. This was late and the troop transports had to move to avoid fire from 8-inch (20-cm) shore guns brought from Singapore, which had survived the first bombardment. Dive-bombers left the fortifications intact and the naval bombardment resumed for another two and a half hours. It seemed impossible that a single defender could have survived the attack.

From then on, almost everything went wrong. The charts used for the landings were old and inaccurate. Butting into a headwind and brisk Japanese fire, the landing craft were prevented from reaching the shore by low tide, coral reefs and Japanese concrete barriers. Japanese guns knocked out the US Amtracs – amphibious personnel carriers – and most troops had to wade ashore. The first wave suffered crippling casualties, and tanks and radio sets were swamped and rendered useless.

Slowly and painfully, the Americans pushed inland. Warships delivered a creeping barrage so close to the leading troops that the Japanese found it impossible to counterattack, and US troops knocked out one strong point after another with explosives and flamethrowers. But poor communications meant the landing was still in doubt at sunset and even with next day's reinforcements, casualties were even higher than before. Only when the tide finally rose, enabling landing craft to reach the shore, did prospects improve. The Japanese kept up heavy fire through the second night but by the afternoon of the third day, resistance had ceased.

The Outcome and Significance

Of the 5,000 Japanese defenders, a single officer, 16 privates and 129 Korean labourers were left alive – all the rest were crushed or burned to death in the bunkers or died in suicide attacks on the invaders.

Seizing bases for airstrips to attack Japan in the Pacific war meant US forces had to overcome formidable Japanese fortifications. Before attacking any more Japanese island bases, the Americans analysed the lessons of Tarawa. In future, bombardments would be longer, with plunging, more damaging fire. Detailed reconnaissance would check tides and underwater obstacles. Improved landing craft, amphibious vehicles and communications would enable the taking of other Japanese bases, including, eventually, the Marianas, which allowed the start of the massive bombing of Japan.

Success of a Seaborne Invasion

Where: Normandy, northern France
When: 1944
War: Second World War (1939–45)
Combatants: Allies vs. Germany
Casualties: Allies: 10,000;
             Germans: 5,000–10,000

Towards the end of the Second World War, carrying out successful landings on the Channel coastline, in the face of the formidable German Army, was a highly hazardous and complex operation. Wherever the Allies chose to land, the result would be affected by how quickly they could reinforce the bridgehead and how quickly the Germans reacted. There were only two real possibilities: the Pas de Calais, which offered both the shortest sea crossing and the shortest land route to Germany; or Normandy, which was further away but less heavily defended. It was essential to keep the Germans guessing for as long as possible, which meant a huge deception operation.

The Positions

The decision was made to land in Normandy, in order to avoid the massive reserves of the German 15th Army in the Pas de Calais. Huge numbers of fake aircraft, tanks, landing craft and massive radio traffic were placed in south-eastern England while the real invasion forces were built up in the south-west. In addition to this, the huge network of German agents captured and turned around on arrival in Britain – reinforced by additional imaginary spies – reported Allied plans to land around Calais. Even when the real landings had taken place, urgent spy messages suggested this was a feint to decoy the 15th Army to Normandy, whereupon the main attack would hit Calais after all.

The Battle

The complex and multilayered deception worked so well that the 15th Army remained where it was. The huge Allied invasion fleet appeared off the

Normandy coast on 6 June 1944 and began unloading landing craft, amphibious tanks and 130,000 troops onto the five invasion beaches. The initial German response depended on the small panzer reserves in the area, which local commanders could not order to counterattack without confirmation from Hitler. By the time orders came, Allied aircraft held them up until their beachheads were firmly established.

However, before the breakout could begin, German reinforcements held up progress, particularly on the eastern, British sector, where the city of Caen – one of the first day's objectives – took weeks of heavy fighting to capture. On the western side of the bridgehead the Americans, after heavy casualties on Omaha Beach in the initial landing, had cut off the Cotentin Peninsula and captured the port of Cherbourg by 26 June. By then, Allied strength in the bridgehead exceeded half a million.

The final breakout began with massive US bombing attacks on 26 July, which almost destroyed an entire panzer division near the town of St. Lo. As the Germans fell back, American tanks and motorized infantry poured through the breach, past the town of Avranches and into open country beyond. Two US armies now fanned out across the French countryside, into Brittany and down the Atlantic coast.

Hitler's reaction was to attack westward, to cut off the American breakout at Avranches. Despite huge efforts, German attacks failed to breach American defences, and laid themselves open to an enormous trap. On 9 August, Patton's troops reached Le Mans and then swung northwards to hit the Germans' left flank, at the same time as the British and Canadians pushed southwards from Caen, striving to meet the Americans near Argentan to close the jaws of the trap.

The Outcome and Significance

More than 15 German divisions were trapped in a pocket 16 kilometres (10 miles) across and 32 kilometres (20 miles) from east to west between Mortain and Falaise. As they struggled eastwards to escape the closing jaws of the Allied armies, British and American aircraft executed a terrible and unopposed slaughter, hitting tanks with rockets and soft-skinned vehicles with bombs and gunfire. Seventy thousand German troops were killed or taken prisoner, but their determined resistance held the jaws of the Allied trap apart for eight vital hours while the rest escaped. Within weeks France was free, and on 11 September American troops crossed the German frontier near Aachen.

The liberation of France was the greatest seaborne invasion in history. No military operation is more hazardous than an opposed landing and, in the case of Normandy, the bitter fighting that followed the original landings paved the way for the ensuing triumph. D-Day showed that the success of an opposed landing rested on the rate at which either side could reinforce the troops initially involved in the fighting. Ultimately a combination of Allied deception and air power proved decisive in preventing German units reaching the battlefront until it was too late.

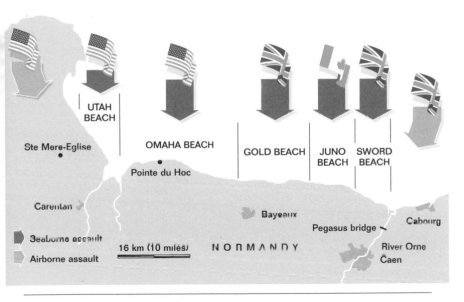

Above Normandy landings on the Northern coast of France. The tactics of deception employed by the Allies allowed the landings to take place successfully.

Part Five:
Modern Wars

The Fortress that Failed

Where: Dien Bien Phu, North Vietnam
When: 1954
War: French Indo–China war (1946–1954)
Combatants: France vs. Vietnam
Casualties: French: 7,500; Vietnamese: 22,000

In 1953, the French wanted to cut their Vietnamese guerrilla opponents' supply lines into Laos. They set up a heavily defended base at Dien Bien Phu, around an airstrip in the northern mountains. Troops were brought in and supplied by air, to ensure a valuable victory before planned peace negotiations.

The Positions

Dien Bien Phu was surrounded by hills but the guerrillas had always previously lacked artillery. The French built seven defensive strongpoints around the airfield, using bulldozers and barbed wire brought in by air. The 10,000-strong garrison was reinforced to 16,000, with light tanks and artillery. However, the Vietnamese reacted far more sharply than predicted, moving in five regular army divisions into the hills, including one artillery division entirely made up of heavy guns. Anti-aircraft guns were hidden close to the airfield and civilian volunteers infiltrated the French positions to pinpoint the French artillery.

The Battle

The first shots were fired on 31 January 1954, and the French found themselves surrounded. The Vietnamese built up supplies in preparation for the full-scale attack. This began on 13 March, with a day-long artillery barrage, followed by a night attack, which took the first French strongpoint.

The French were appalled at the accuracy and intensity of enemy gunfire. They were even more shocked at their own inability to silence the enemy guns. The Vietnamese placed guns individually rather than in batteries, firing from specially excavated tunnels, and each gun crew did its own spotting and aiming. Though less efficient than orthodox tactics, this proved devastatingly effective at Dien Bien Phu, since the Vietnamese knew the exact position of each French

Right French paratroopers land in Dien Bien Phu on 23 March 1954, the start of the 55-day siege.

gun, while the French had no similar information. The Vietnamese even concealed the muzzle flashes of their guns and moved regularly between sites, replacing guns with wooden replicas.

Vietnamese artillery silenced the French guns, rendered the airstrip unusable and pounded each strongpoint before the infantry attacked. They dug more than 320 kilometres (200 miles) of trenches, encircling the French defences. As the French perimeter shrank, the air supply drops fell more on Vietnamese positions than French and aircraft losses increased under anti-aircraft fire. By 7 May, most central positions had fallen.

The Outcome and Significance

The fall of Dien Bien Phu meant the end of French Indo-China. Having lost one-tenth of their army in Vietnam, the French had to ask for an armistice at the Geneva Peace Conference of 1954, which was followed by their withdrawal.

Dien Bien Phu represented a huge escalation in a classic guerrilla campaign. Normally, these would end with the wearing down of one side or another over years of fighting. In this case, the French attempt to provoke a pitched battle rebounded as the Vietnamese evolved overnight from a guerrilla force into an army capable of fighting – and beating – a Western army equipped with modern weapons. However, it cost them three times the French casualties to do so.

The Media in Warfare

Where: Saigon, South Vietnam
When: 1968
War: Vietnam War (1959–1975)
Combatants: America vs. North Vietnam
Casualties: Americans and allies: 27,000;
              Vietnamese: 75,000

On 31 January 1968, at the Vietnamese New Year holiday (Tet), rebel Vietnamese forces attacked cities, towns and villages across South Vietnam to try to win a final victory over the Americans before increasing damage suffered by their own side made this impossible. The date was chosen for maximum surprise, as both sides had agreed a truce over the holiday.

The Positions

After attempts to draw the Americans and their allies away from the cities, more than 85,000 guerrillas, backed up by 130,000 North Vietnamese Army troops, struck more than 100 cities, towns and villages all over the South, hoping to spark an uprising and end the war on their own terms. At first, surprise proved effective, but within days the Americans and South Vietnamese had begun the long battle to re-establish control.

The Battle

In the capital, Saigon, the Viet Cong seized the presidential palace, the army headquarters, the airport and the grounds of the US Embassy but American and South Vietnamese troops had retaken all these objectives within a week. Elsewhere, regaining control took longer. In the old Vietnamese imperial capital of Hue, the attackers held on to their gains. It took massive US and South Vietnamese firepower to take the city in over three weeks of heavy fighting, during which time the historic centre was almost totally destroyed. Thousands of civilians died in the fighting and more than 100,000 lost their homes.

The major US base of Khe Sanh was attacked by 20,000 North Vietnamese regulars 10 days before the main offensive, and large reinforcements were rushed to the area to prevent another Dien Bien Phu (see page 104). Similarities included huge artillery duels between the Americans and North Vietnamese, but here massive US air raids dropped almost 40,000 tons of bombs on the enemy to blunt their attacks. Once again rebel anti-aircraft guns threatened supply drops, but fighter-bomber escorts attacked the gun positions and the missions were successful until, finally, a relieving force reached the base on 8 April. While later phases of the battle against different targets lasted over most of May and from mid-August to mid-September, here, too, rebel casualties mounted. Even where they made encouraging initial gains, they consistently underestimated the mobility of their opponents, who were able to counterattack in massive numbers, quickly and effectively.

The Outcome and Significance

The campaign was a clear military defeat for the North Vietnamese and Viet Cong. Against American and South Vietnamese casualties of just over 4,300 killed, 16,000 wounded and more than 1,000 missing, they lost between 75,000 and 85,000 killed in action, mostly attacking large units in well-defended positions. This was the classic fate for guerrillas fighting a regular army in pitched battle and the gamble seemed lost.

The Tet offensive was a North Vietnamese attempt to seize the initiative from the Americans and South Vietnamese, as they had done with the French at Dien Bien Phu. This meant a much larger scale operation, and the powerful US forces in Vietnam were bound to defeat any guerrilla force, however highly committed. Yet the world's first media-covered battle transformed the North Vietnamese defeat into victory, through dwindling support for the war at home, owing mainly to the impact of graphic images of the fighting beamed into family homes on nightly television news broadcasts.

Shock and Firepower

Where:	Kuwait and Iraq	
When:	1991	
War:	First Gulf War (1990–1991)	
Combatants:	Coalition forces vs. Iraq	
Casualties:	Coalition: 800; Iraqis: estimates range between 20,000–200,000	

Following Saddam Hussein's invasion of Kuwait on 2 August 1990, a massive coalition was massed under UN auspices to prevent moves into Saudi Arabia. As pressure to persuade the Iraqis to withdraw proved unsuccessful, the coalition forces planned a military offensive to retake Kuwaiti territory. Given Iraq's huge military resources, this promised to be an expensive and bloody operation.

The Positions

By January 1991, when the attack was about to be launched, coalition forces in the area included six US Navy carrier battle groups and two battleships launching cruise missiles, along with massive ground and air forces. The Iraqis had only small inshore naval forces, and nearly half the coalition's 1,800 aircraft, but rumours spoke of more than a million troops and 5,000 tanks to outnumber coalition forces. Most were dug in along the Iraqi border and seemed to present a genuine challenge to attacking forces.

The Battle

Operation Desert Storm began on 17 January 1991 with huge air strikes over Iraq. Waves of stealth bombers, helicopters and remotely piloted drones targeted Iraqi air defence radars, power supply installations and surface-to-air missile sites, rendering air defence powerless in many areas.

As ground forces moved to attack on 24 February, the gap in technology between Iraqi forces and the coalition became obvious, as the coalition had precision-guided cruise missiles and 'smart' laser-guided bombs to hit key targets. By the end of the campaign, 96 per cent of Iraq's electrical generating capacity had been destroyed.

A deception scheme suggested the coalition forces planned a seaborne landing from the Gulf to outflank the Iraqi defensive line from the east. In fact, large reserves built up in the west advanced into the desert to move in a classic left-hook around the exposed Iraqi right flank, before swinging around to the east and attacking the elite Republican Guard armoured units. Because of coalition satellite navigation systems, their units could navigate accurately and in darkness across trackless desert to target known enemy forces.

The Outcome and Significance

After four days of fighting, the campaign was over, with Iraqi casualties so massive that the true figures remain unknown. The Iraqi defences did succeed in two areas. They used electric heaters and dummy tanks to distract heat-seeking missiles and they used low-level anti-aircraft weapons to bring down coalition aircraft. In all other respects, coalition forces inflicted a massive defeat with heavy casualties for the price of 181 coalition personnel killed by enemy fire, in an awesome demonstration of the power of modern weapons.

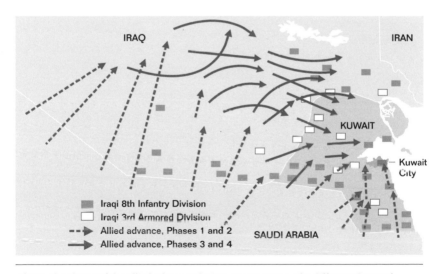

Above The phases of the Allied advances during Desert Storm. The different phases of advance allowed the Allied forces to outflank the Iraqi Army.

Part Six:
Naval War

New Naval Tactics

Where: English Channel and British coast
When: 1588
War: Spanish invasion campaign (1588)
Combatants: England vs. Spain
Casualties: English: 500; Spanish:
             16,000–22,000

King Philip II of Spain wanted to restore England to the Catholic faith and eliminate English piracy on Spanish trade. He decided to invade England, sailing an Armada into the Channel to carry a Spanish army from the Netherlands to land in Kent.

The Positions

Philip's colossal fleet included 130 ships from Spain, the Baltic, Portugal and Italy, carrying more than 20,000 troops. Having halted for repairs from storm damage, it finally sailed from Lisbon on 28 May 1588, but by then the English knew it was coming.

In battle, the Spanish used medieval naval tactics, firing a single, close-range broadside at an opponent before boarding so that their troops could capture the enemy ship. Since the gun crews took part in the attack, they never practised loading and firing repeated broadsides. Instead, the English used smaller, lower, faster and more manoeuvrable ships, thanks to more efficient rigging, which could dash in and out to fire repeated broadsides without being boarded and seized.

The Battle

The Armada was sighted early on the misty morning of 19 July 1588 off the Lizard Peninsula near the tip of Cornwall. Blazing beacons relayed the news to London and the English fleet sailed as soon as the tide served. On the night of 20 July the fleets sighted one another near the Eddystone Rocks off Plymouth and the English approached from upwind, allowing them to harass the Spanish at will. At first, their new tactics produced a stalemate. The

Spanish adopted a crescent-shaped formation, which protected their most vulnerable ships and made them difficult to attack. Firing at Spanish rigging caused trivial damage and the stout construction of the larger Spanish ships made them tough targets. Only two Spanish ships were lost – one after a collision and the other after an internal explosion – but the Armada now faced a greater problem.

Although expected to ferry troops from Holland to England, the Armada lacked pilots to guide it through the complicated approaches to the Dutch ports, so it had to anchor in open water off Gravelines near Calais on 28 July. Here it proved fatally vulnerable to another English tactic: fire ships. Old vessels set ablaze by their skeleton crews, these drifted downwind towards anchored enemy vessels, setting them on fire. The Spanish managed to board and divert one fire ship, but another seven forced the rest of their fleet to cut their cables and flee. The English fleet was waiting and this time the Spaniards' lack of formation allowed the English to close the range with their opponents and sink two ships by repeated broadsides, leaving the rest to flee north-eastwards.

The Outcome and Significance

Spanish invasion plans had been defeated and weather and geography would all but destroy their Armada. Forced to sail right around Britain without charts and through the most treacherous of waters, many ships were wrecked on the rocky coasts of Scotland and Ireland and only half managed to return home.

Though storms and shipwreck destroyed far more ships than the English fleet, its role had been instrumental in thwarting the Armada's purpose, and forcing it to adopt its terrible escape route. In the longer term, their tactics of skilled ship handling, with repeated broadsides to beat an opponent into submission became the foundation of naval tactics for more than 200 years and provided England's naval supremacy for most of that period.

Royal Navy's Deadly Fire

Where: Cape Trafalgar, Spanish coast
When: 1805
War: Napoleonic War (1803–1815)
Combatants: Britain vs. France and Spain
Casualties: British: 449;
            French and Spanish: 3,250

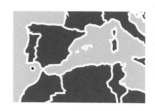

At the battle of Cape St. Vincent in February 1797, Nelson stopped the Spanish escaping by using his ship, HMS *Captain,* to board and capture two much larger Spanish ships, an astonishing achievement. A year later, he caught a French fleet at anchor in Aboukir Bay near Alexandria. Because the ships could not escape, Nelson's fleet captured or destroyed almost all of them. Could he now use the same tactics on the open sea in the Battle of Trafalgar?

The Positions

In October 1805, early on in the Napoleonic War, the main French and Spanish fleets of 33 ships of the line emerged from Cadiz to find Nelson and his 27 ships waiting for them. Admiral Villeneuve, the fleet commander, immediately turned back to port, but this manoeuvre caused his fleet to form a straggling double line, with French and Spanish ships intermingled, in light and fickle winds. Immediately Nelson steered for his prey.

The Battle

Sailing warships carried their guns in batteries along the sides of the ship, making them most vulnerable to enemy broadsides from ahead or astern. Their own guns could not reply and enemy shot could 'rake' the length of a ship, causing far more damage than firing broadside to broadside. Consequently, no commander would ever willingly expose his ship to raking fire.

Yet Nelson planned to do exactly this. He divided his fleet into two columns, to break the enemy line in two places and prevent its retreat. In light winds, his ships would close the enemy at walking pace, suffering the raking fire of their broadsides for more than half an hour without being able to reply. Only after running this terrible gauntlet could they fire back at last. The result of this ordeal was a victory as powerful as even Nelson could have wished. His ships endured crippling enemy fire until noon, when Admiral Collingwood, leading the southern column in HMS *Royal Sovereign*, broke through the enemy line. Nelson, leading the northern column in HMS *Victory*, followed suit almost 45 minutes later. As the British ships passed the enemy vessels, they had their revenge at last, raking them in turn before turning alongside and bringing their own broadsides into play. Given the greater experience and the deadly fire of Royal Navy gun crews, this won the battle.

The Outcome and Significance

Nelson's triumph cost him his life, as a sharpshooter in the rigging fired a single mortal shot. Before he died, Nelson knew 18 enemy ships had been taken or sunk, with no British ship lost. Nelson's crushing victory prevented Napoleon seizing command of the English Channel, which was essential for his plans to invade England and eliminate his deadliest enemy.

Trafalgar had allowed the Royal Navy to deploy its superb seamanship and deadly gunnery in crushing an opponent. This victory meant no potential enemy was willing to build and equip a fleet to mount a serious challenge for more than a century. When it did, in the age of ironclad steamships, Nelson's tactics of approaching and breaking the enemy line would have been impossible against enemy broadsides of heavy guns firing explosive shells.

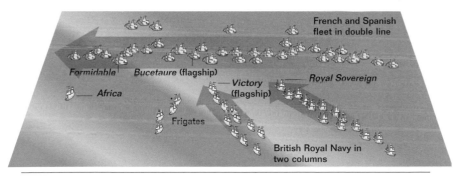

Above The two columns of Nelson's fleet close in on the Spanish and French ships.

A Key Role for Battleships

Where: Tsushima Strait, Sea of Japan
When: 1905
War: Russo–Japanese War (1904–1905)
Combatants: Russia vs. Japan
Casualties: Russian: 10,000; Japanese: 700

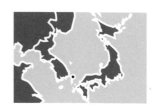

At the beginning of the 19th century, hostilities between Russia and Japan over Russian expansion in the Far East led to successful Japanese invasions of Korea and Russian territory in Manchuria. Russian naval forces in the area suffered several defeats and, in October 1904, Russia sent its Baltic Fleet on an epic voyage around the world to crush the Japanese.

The Positions

In early May 1905, the Russian fleet reached the China Sea. Though it contained an apparently formidable force of 11 battleships, 6 cruisers and a total of 45 vessels – seemingly a match for its Japanese opponents – most of the ships were old and relatively slow and their crews poorly trained. The seven-month voyage involved refuelling several times, leaving piles of coal on the upper decks, as the ships sailed through the misty Straits of Tsushima between the Japanese islands and the coast of South Korea, the most direct route to their base at Vladivostok.

The Battle

At 04.45 on 27 May, a Japanese auxiliary cruiser, the *Shinano Maru*, spotted the Russian ships and signalled naval headquarters. Within two hours the battle fleet had sailed, and at 13.40, sighted the Russians. The Japanese were on a westerly heading with their heaviest battleships in the lead, followed by armoured cruisers; to attack the enemy heading north-east, they needed to reverse their line. Rather than turn all ships together, reversing the sequence, Admiral Togo risked Russian fire by turning his ships one after the other as they reached a given spot, risking its being targeted by enemy gunners. The Russians missed their chance, however, and the faster Japanese ships drew ahead of their adversaries while both sides commenced firing. Finally, the Japanese crossed the enemy's course in a manoeuvre called 'crossing the T', which allowed their ships to fire broadsides, while the Russians could only reply with their bow turrets.

From the beginning, the contest was unequal. The Japanese had better range-finders and more practised crews. They used high-explosive shells to blast the superstructure of the Russian ships and set the piles of coal on fire. The Russian guns used armour-piercing shells but the fuses proved unreliable. One by one, their ships fell victim to the merciless Japanese fire. After half an hour, two of the Russian battleships – one of them the flagship – were ablaze and a third was leaving the battle line. By dusk, after the fleets had passed one another again, the Japanese had sunk three Russian battleships and had hit a fourth, the *Borodino*, in her magazine, blowing her to pieces.

At around 20.00, the Japanese sent in torpedo boats and destroyers to attack the crippled Russian fleet. One battleship hit a mine and stopped, to be sunk by torpedoes, while the Russians scuttled another the following morning along with two armoured cruisers. Finally, four of the remaining five battleships surrendered, while the Japanese sunk the fifth. Only three small Russian ships reached Vladivostok.

The Outcome and Significance

The victory was as decisive as Trafalgar had been a century before (see page 114). Though the financial strain of the war brought Japan near to collapse, Tsushima forced Russia to agree peace terms.

This triumphant battleship duel underlined the value of a navy to the increasingly aggressive Japan. Although her Imperial Navy would use aircraft carriers as a powerful new weapon in the Second World War, sufficient senior admirals remained convinced after Tsushima that battleships were still the truly decisive weapon – a false doctrine that affected naval planning and made eventual defeat inevitable.

Pre-emptive Strikes

Where: Pearl Harbor, Hawaii, USA
When: 1941
War: Second World War (1939–1945)
Combatants: America vs. Japan
Casualties: Americans: 2,300; Japanese: 65

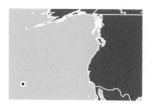

In the early 1940s, worsening relations with the United States and tightening embargoes threatened Japanese war plans in South-east Asia. They believed attacking Malaya would provoke retaliation by the US Pacific Fleet from its Hawaii base, so they decided to eliminate the threat by a carrier strike.

The Positions

Six Japanese carriers with more than 400 aircraft sailed from their bases on 26 November 1941 into seas north of Hawaii, while negotiations continued. The Japanese planned to declare war half an hour before the attack but delays meant the attack would arrive first. Meanwhile, Pearl Harbor's peacetime routine continued in ignorance. The battleships were moored in pairs alongside Ford Island, with two heavy carriers absent, USS *Enterprise* and USS *Lexington*, which were ferrying fighters to Wake Island and Midway. On airfields, aircraft were marshalled in lines to guard against saboteurs, ideal for strafing raiders.

The Battle

The Japanese strike force approached within 320 kilometres (200 miles) of Hawaii without being spotted, a feat for which carrier ships were vital, and at 06.00 on 7 December 1941 they began launching their planes. The first attack wave of 183 aircraft was equipped with torpedoes, while the second wave of 170 bombers would attack targets that remained undamaged, with the escorting fighters shooting up the airfields to keep defending fighters from taking off. By 07.52 they reached Hawaii.

The defences were woefully unprepared, with ammunition stores locked and guns unmanned but individuals reacted with speed and courage. A handful of fighters managed to take off between bomb bursts and anti-aircraft guns began peppering the sky with shells. Nevertheless, by the end of the attacks, the Japanese had sunk 5 battleships and 13 other vessels and had destroyed or damaged more than four-fifths of the aircraft on the island.

The Outcome and Significance

Despite winning a spectacular victory, vital targets had been missed, including dockyard facilities, the submarine base, which would play a crucial role in destroying the Japanese merchant fleet and the intelligence centre, which broke Japanese ciphers. But their most fatal omission was missing the two US carriers at sea, which would help turn the tables at Midway the following summer and make American victory inevitable (see page 120).

Japan achieved total surprise in their devastating pre-emptive strike on Pearl Harbor. The attack owed much to the British carrier strike against the Italian fleet at Taranto in November 1940, when antiquated Swordfish biplanes crippled two Italian battleships. It underlined the strategy of power projection, using carriers to strike at targets beyond the range of shore-based aircraft, but also emphasized the need for target intelligence to ensure strikes were effective.

Above The USS *Arizona*, destroyed during the Japanese attack on Pearl Harbor.

Ships of the Future

Where: Midway Island, central Pacific
When: 1942
War: Second World War (1939–1945)
Combatants: America vs. Japan
Casualties: Americans: 300; Japanese: 3,000

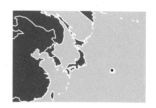

Following their attack on Pearl Harbor, and their successful invasions of
Malaya, the Philippines and the Dutch East Indies, the next Japanese Navy
priority was to attack the US base at Midway Island, 1,600 kilometres (1,000
miles) west of Hawaii. They developed a complex attack plan, including
diversionary attacks as far north as the Aleutians, but US code-breakers soon
revealed the enemy's true intentions.

The Positions

The Japanese believed they could deliver a surprise attack on the island with
four carriers on 4 June 1942 and land troops two days later, before the
Americans reacted. However, warned by their code-breakers, the three
available US carriers, USS *Enterprise*, USS *Lexington*, and USS *Yorktown* had
rendezvoused 560 kilometres (350 miles) north-east of Midway and were
searching for the Japanese carriers *Akagi*, *Hiryu*, *Soryu* and *Kaga*, then some
640 kilometres (400 miles) to their west. The Japanese had no idea of the
whereabouts of the US carriers, but were searching for them to sink them as
quickly as possible.

The Battle

Before dawn on 4 June the first wave of Japanese planes took off to attack
Midway. At the same time, a Midway-based scout plane sighted the Japanese
carriers and radioed their position to the US fleet. Worried their own carriers
might be seen by Japanese search planes, the Americans launched a strike
against the enemy, even though the targets were at the limit of their range. By
09.00, 156 American fighters, torpedo bombers and dive-bombers were heading
for the Japanese fleet. They finally found their targets in a state of confusion.

After the Midway attack planes had left, the Japanese reserve aircraft had been assembled on the flight decks, armed with torpedoes ready to attack the American carriers as soon as these were found. In the meantime, shore-based aircraft from Midway had delivered ineffective attacks against the Japanese ships and the Japanese commander decided to rearm the planes on deck with bombs, ready for a follow-up attack against Midway instead. This had just been completed when a Japanese scout plane reported the position of at least one US carrier, just as the first strike planes returned from Midway, needing to refuel and rearm.

Faced with the need to switch back to torpedoes for the second strike planes, and send them below for the first strike planes to land back on deck, the bombs were stacked on deck and in the hangars and fuel lines spread across the decks to refuel as quickly as possible. At that moment the first American strike planes arrived, torpedo bombers attacking at low level. Furious anti-aircraft fire and Zero fighters from the carriers' defensive patrols managed to shoot them all down without any damage to the carriers.

Right The Second World War first saw aircraft carriers playing a key role as a seagoing airbase, allowing a naval force to project air power great distances without having to depend on local bases.

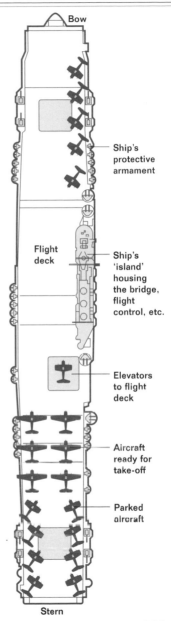

Bow

Ship's protective armament

Flight deck

Ship's 'island' housing the bridge, flight control, etc.

Elevators to flight deck

Aircraft ready for take-off

Parked aircraft

Stern

However, at that very moment, with the Japanese frantically preparing to launch their own strike against the US carriers, the course of the Pacific war was changed in just five short minutes. The second wave of the American strike – their high-level dive-bombers – arrived over the targets a few minutes late, to find the Japanese defending fighters all down at sea level. They began their diving (and highly accurate) attacks unopposed by enemy aircraft, on ships awash with fuel and ammunition and the results were cataclysmic. The *Kaga, Akagi* and *Soryu* were set ablaze from end to end and only the *Hiryu* was left to launch its own strike, following the returning American aircraft to hit the USS *Yorktown* with bombs and torpedoes. Despite desperate efforts to keep her afloat, a Japanese submarine sunk her by torpedo two days later. In retribution, American planes from the other two carriers found the *Hiryu* on 5 June and wrecked her, leaving her to be sunk by Japanese destroyers a day later to prevent her falling into enemy hands.

The Outcome and Significance

The Japanese Navy never recovered from the loss of four large carriers but it paid an even heavier price in the loss of 3,500 trained aircrew and their planes. Against American industrial might and the rapidly increasing carrier strength of the US Navy, this shortage of trained and experienced aircrew was never remedied and made Japanese defeat inevitable.

Carriers had shown themselves to be the capital ships of the future – but already carrier operations were clearly dependent on good intelligence and good communications to find the enemy and launch strikes effectively. Without these advantages, the carriers remained deeply vulnerable to being attacked and sunk in turn.

U-boat Stranglehold

Where: Mid-Atlantic Ocean
When: 1943
War: Second World War (1939–1945)
Combatants: Allies vs. Germany
Casualties: Allies: 80,000; Germany: 19,000

In both world wars, the German Navy tried to impose a submarine blockade to prevent supplies reaching Britain. In the first war, the Allies grouped ships into convoys which proved decisive in reducing losses but in the second, the conquest of France enabled the Germans to set up U-boat bases along the Biscay coast, much closer to the convoy routes, to exert a terrible toll on merchant ships.

The Positions

By early 1943, German 'wolf-pack' tactics were working effectively. Patrol lines of U-boats would spread out across the convoy routes to extend their visibility as far as possible. As soon as a convoy was located, the rest of the pack would be radioed in to attack. Surface escorts were in short supply and the mid-Atlantic air gap, out of range of shore-based patrol aircraft, gave U-boat crews relatively easy hunting. The struggle reached its climax in March 1943, when a scouting U-boat spotted the spark of a cigarette being lit on a merchant ship's deck one pitch-black night, leading to attacks on three convoys and the loss of 22 ships totalling 146,000 tons for the loss of a single U-boat.

Desperate situations bring radical measures and already plans were in hand to divert more long-range aircraft to anti-submarine duties and more warships to reinforce the hard-pressed escorts. By the following month, a slow westbound convoy, ONS5, began its crossing on 22 April, facing terrible weather and the largest concentration of U-boats ever recorded. With 40 merchant ships, protected by just 7 small escort vessels, it faced a terrible challenge and a massacre seemed inevitable. But massive help was on its way at last.

The Battle

The weather struck first on 26 April, with storms forcing many lightly loaded ships out of position and causing two to collide. Two days later, the first U-boat picked up convoy sounds on hydrophones and called in 14 others. Later that day, Allied escorts detected and attacked two submarines approaching from the windward side – the escort commander decided attacks could not be made from the starboard, leeward side in the mountainous seas and sent all his escorts to the port side to deter each attack with depth charges. By 2 May, the Germans had torpedoed just one merchant ship, but the rough weather stopped many escorts from topping up fuel tanks from the convoy and several had to run for harbour while they could still manoeuvre.

Above German Type VII U-Boat U-570, which was forced to surrender by a Hudson aircraft of RAF Coastal Command, being brought into a British port.

To deal with the situation, four Home Fleet destroyers joined the Allies' convoy and formed a patrol line ahead of its leading ships to force any shadowing U-boats to dive deep and risk losing contact. On 4 May, three of these destroyers had to leave the convoy to refuel and the weather was easing at a time when 30 U-boats were known to be homing in. By 5 May, the first had arrived and no less than 11 merchant ships were torpedoed, though another escort group was on its way to reinforce the beleaguered convoy. During that night, a total of 24 U-boat attacks were made on the convoy, with the devoted escorts driving off every one of them. The Allies sunk four U-boats and damaged another three heavily enough to keep them out of the battle and no more merchantmen were lost. On the morning of 6 May, the new escort group joined the convoy, driving off several more U-boats and sinking another one. Two more collided and sank and another had been spotted and sunk by a patrol plane. Later that morning the U-boats were called off.

The Outcome and Significance

Convoy ONS5 presented the German U-boats with perhaps their ideal target, attracting between 51 and 70 submarines to attack a small group of slow-moving merchantmen. They inflicted heavy losses, sinking 12 ships, but had lost 8 submarines and damaged 2 more – an unacceptable rate of exchange – showing how completely the pendulum had swung back in favour of the Allies in a month of the Atlantic battle.

Though the war still had two years to run, never again did U-boats present a real threat. Increasing numbers of escorts and patrol planes with sophisticated radars and weapons like homing torpedoes made the Atlantic lethal for German submariners. By the end of the war in May 1945, three U-boat men out of four had been killed in action in this long and bitter battle, but post-war nuclear submarines would be much harder to sink in any future trade war.

Long-distance Landing

Where: Falkland Islands, South Atlantic
When: 1982
War: Falklands War (1982)
Combatants: Britain vs. Argentina
Casualties: British: 255;
            Argentinians: 649

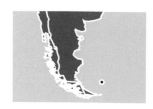

Following Argentine landings on the Falkland Islands, on 2 April 1982, the decision to expel the invaders meant sending a naval task force all the way to the South Atlantic and mounting a successful seaborne landing within range of Argentine shore-based aircraft – one of the most difficult military operations in the depths of the southern winter.

The Positions

As the task force neared its objective within weeks of the Argentine landings, they faced threats from both Argentine warships and aircraft. For troops to land on the relatively sheltered beaches bordering San Carlos Water between West and East Falkland, the British sent in smaller frigates and destroyers to defend against Argentine air raids and warn the aircraft carriers, HMS *Hermes* and HMS *Invincible*, stationed further to the east.

The Battle

The first part of the naval operation began with the arrival of the nuclear-powered attack submarine HMS *Conqueror* in the area on 19 April, followed by a Royal Marine force, which retook the island of South Georgia on 25 April. *Santa Fe*, an Argentine submarine, was attacked by ships' helicopters on the same day, leaving it unable to dive and forcing it ashore on the island. A week later, *Conqueror* spotted the Argentine cruiser *General Belgrano* and sank it with torpedoes in what remains a controversial action. Its immediate effect was the retreat of all other Argentine Navy vessels into port and the *General Belgrano*'s commander said later that he regarded the attack as a legitimate wartime option.

For the remainder of the campaign, the Argentines attacked with aircraft. Mirage fighters and Skyhawk fighter-bombers used bombs and Exocet missiles to try to sink or damage the British carriers. These remained out of reach but their Sea Harrier fighters shot down several Argentine aircraft in the opening days of the campaign. Sea Harriers also dropped cluster bombs to reinforce the damage caused to the Port Stanley airstrip by ultra-long range RAF Vulcan raids, rendering it unusable for high-performance jets.

Later Argentine raids became more deadly as they began approaching below radar coverage, climbing to allow their missile radars to lock on to their chosen targets, and then firing before retiring below the radar again. Air-launched Exocet missiles sank HMS *Sheffield*, a type 42 destroyer, on 4 May from a range of more than 32 kilometres (20 miles), and the supply ship *Atlantic Conveyor* on 25 May. Other losses included the frigates HMS *Ardent* and HMS *Antelope*, struck by Argentine bombs on May 21 and the destroyer HMS *Coventry* four days later. Losses would have been heavier if Argentine aircraft had been able to bomb from higher altitude, allowing the fuses on their bombs to activate fully.

The Outcome and Significance

The sacrifices of the smaller naval vessels preserved the carriers and the fleet's own air cover for the remainder of the campaign. Troops landed on East Falkland on the night of 21 May and following the battle of Goose Green and Darwin against nearby Argentine posts, began moving east to attack the main Argentine positions guarding the capital, Port Stanley. British reinforcements arrived on 1 June, and two weeks later the Argentine forces surrendered. The war had lasted 74 days and cost the lives of 649 Argentine servicemen against those of 255 British.

The battle of the Falklands remains almost unique as a seaborne landing successfully carried out thousands of miles from the nearest friendly base. However, it underlined the need for heavier anti-aircraft weapons for surface ships and early-warning radar aircraft to monitor incoming air raids.

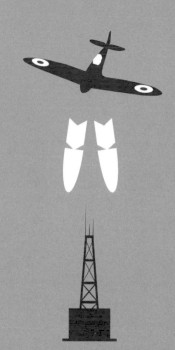

Part Seven:
Aerial Battles

First Long-range Aerial Bombing

Where: South-eastern England
When: 1915
War: First World War (1914–1918)
Combatants: Britain vs. Germany
Casualties: British: more than 300;
                Germans: 77 airships destroyed

In 1915, Germany achieved a feat that had eluded Britain's enemies for
centuries: outflanking the English Channel's natural obstacle to strike at the
heart of the enemy nation. The means was the airship, floating above its
targets and dropping bombs with apparent impunity.

The Positions

Initially, the Germans used their Zeppelins for reconnaissance, such as
plotting the movements of British minelayers and relaying details of the
resulting minefields to German shipping. However, their reliance on
hydrogen for lift, and their resulting vulnerability to incendiary bullets,
led the German Navy to develop airships into a serious weapon of war.
Finally, searching for a new way of striking at his enemies, the Kaiser
approved Zeppelin raids against military sites on the British mainland in
January 1915.

The Battle

The first raid on Britain was launched on 19 January, but an effective
blackout prevented the airship crews from finding military targets, leaving
them to drop bombs and incendiaries on towns and villages in East Anglia,
killing four civilians. They carried out 19 further raids during the year,
against predominantly civilian targets, dropping 37 tons of bombs, and
killing 181 people. Increasing public concern triggered a rush to develop
effective defences. Naval searchlights were adapted for use by the police, to
light up the sky and illuminate the ghostly dirigibles and the first anti-aircraft
guns were relatively small caliber 10-cm (4-inch) weapons.

The decisive defence weapon would be the fighter but at this early stage in the war single-seat fighters lacked a synchronized machine gun that was able to fire through the airscrew arc without hitting the whirling propeller blades. For the time being, the best expedient seemed to be for the fighters to fly above the slow and bulky airships and drop small bombs on them and this finally proved effective – over Ghent rather than England – on 7 June 1915, when Flight Sublieutenant Warneford of the Royal Naval Air Service destroyed a Zeppelin he had chased from Ostend, with the last of his 20-pound (9 kg) bombs. He was awarded the Victoria Cross, but died 10 days later in a flying accident.

This eventually proved to be the nemesis of the night Zeppelin raids. In May 1916 a Zeppelin bombed London by mistake, after which permission was given to target towns and cities deliberately. In 23 raids during the year a further 125 tons of bombs were dropped, killing almost 300 people, but better defences meant that the airships had to seek cloud cover at higher altitudes, finding their targets by lowering observers through the cloud layers. Unfortunately, higher altitudes of up to 3,600 metres (12,000 feet) meant stronger winds, which often scattered the cumbersome craft far from their targets. Finally, increasingly effective fighters with synchronized, forward-firing machine guns delivering bursts of incendiary bullets, began inflicting increasing losses: two airships were brought down in September 1916 and the remaining two years of the war saw just 11 more raids over England, from London to Edinburgh and as far inland as the Midlands.

The Outcome and Significance

By First World War standards, the death toll of the Zeppelin raids was trivial but the campaign was effective in forcing Britain to divert 12 squadrons of fighters – badly needed over the Western Front – and more than 10,000 troops to man the searchlight, gun and air defences.

The Zeppelin campaign was a powerful advance warning of the impact of air power on civilian populations, which would be underlined with much deadlier effect with bomber aircraft in the Second World War. Already the main elements were all in place, from the defences of searchlights and night fighters, to the difficulty of finding military objectives causing the switch to larger, civilian targets.

Radar's Key Role

Where: South-eastern England
When: 1940
War: Second World War (1939–1945)
Combatants: Britain vs. Germany
Casualties: British: 544 airmen, some 27,000
              civilians; Germans: approx 2,500

Germany's conquest of France gave it airfields within range of southern England. Bombers could raid England in daylight escorted by fighters and were able to locate targets and bomb them accurately. They believed superior numbers and experience would defeat the RAF, either enabling an invasion or forcing peace negotiations. The result was the epic Battle of Britain.

The Positions

German bombers could reach as far north as Liverpool, but their fighters could only stay for a short time before running short of fuel. Initially, the Luftwaffe hoped to force the RAF to fly wasteful standing patrols to meet incoming raids. However, they failed to realize that British radar gave enough warning to send up interceptors as each raid approached. The German Bf109 was fast and manoeuvrable and flown by experienced pilots but RAF fighters proved tough opponents: the slower, but rugged, Hurricanes attacked the bombers, while the faster Spitfires tackled German fighters.

The Battle

The battle began with massed attacks from 13 August, mainly against RAF airfields, until bad weather from August 18 brought a lull. The Germans found their Junkers 87 dive-bombers were especially vulnerable to fighter attack and they stopped their tentative attacks on British radar stations.

Right Two types of radar were used on the coast of Britain during the Second World War; Chain Home stations provided long-range detection, while Chain Home Low was shorter-ranged but could detect aircraft flying at lower levels.

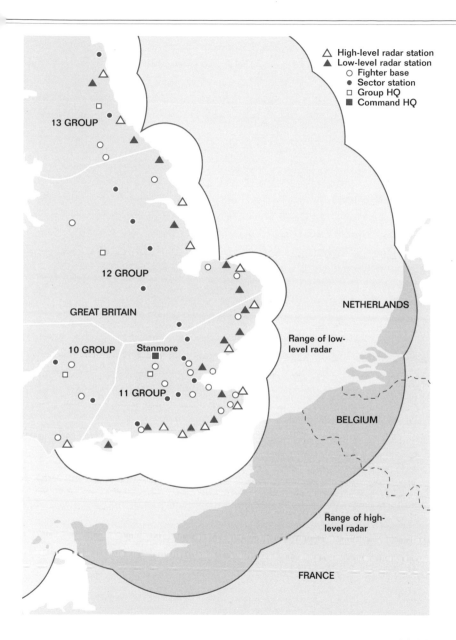

High-level radar station
Low-level radar station
Fighter base
Sector station
Group HQ
Command HQ

13 GROUP

12 GROUP

GREAT BRITAIN

10 GROUP

Stanmore

11 GROUP

NETHERLANDS

Range of low-level radar

BELGIUM

Range of high-level radar

FRANCE

German bomber crew morale plummeted, with no apparent end to RAF attacks on their formations. German fighters were ordered to stay close to the bombers, which meant foregoing their usual advantages of speed, height and attacking out of the sun and increased fuel consumption cut their endurance over England still further. Their only hope was attrition, fighting until the RAF ran out of planes and pilots.

British fighters were produced in large numbers but pilots were in much shorter supply and with the airfields as main targets, they were suffering heavy damage. Believing victory was within its grasp, the Luftwaffe broadened its range of targets to include industry and a raid on 24 August set much of London's East End ablaze. The following night, RAF bombers struck Berlin and, from 5 September, Hitler ordered a shift to attacking cities.

Two days later, the Luftwaffe gave the RAF airfields the respite they desperately needed with a massive late afternoon raid on London by 400 bombers and 600 fighters. The attack confused the defenders, who failed to disrupt the raid, and it went on into the night with bombers aiming at the East End fires. On September 15, they returned in daylight with just 100 bombers, escorted by 400 fighters. This time, the RAF had enough warning to assemble 300 fighters over Kent and Sussex and almost 200 over London. They shot down more than 60 Luftwaffe aircraft – a graphic reinforcement of RAF fighter strength that shattered German morale.

The Outcome and Significance

The battle was effectively over, with the Luftwaffe turning to night raids by bombers and tip-and-run raids by fighters carrying a single bomb apiece. Any threat of invasion vanished and most of the Luftwaffe was finally transferred east for the invasion of Russia on 22 June 1941.

The Battle of Britain proved the impossibility of daylight bombing without long-range fighter escort in the face of resolute defenders. The Germans failed to realize the vital importance of radar in conserving British strength by avoiding the need to keep fighters airborne in wasteful standing patrols. They could have knocked out the stations by bombing their power supplies, as was done in the Gulf War, and this was part of their more widespread lack of good target information.

Hamburg Firestorm

Where: Hamburg, Germany
When: 1943
War: Second World War (1939–1945)
Combatants: Britain vs. Germany
Casualties: British: approx 1,000 airmen
            Germans: approx 50,000 civilians

The night bombing of Germany was Britain's only possible retaliation for much of the war. At first, bombers had difficulty finding targets but increasing strength and new navigation and marking aids brought improvements. By 1943, heavier raids spurred the Germans to develop radar-controlled night fighters to find and shoot down bombers and air fighting over Germany claimed much higher casualties on both sides. Finally, by summer 1943, the RAF held two trump cards: centimetric radar, or H2S, which showed crews a rough map display of the area below the bomber, and 'Window', strips of metalized paper that could be dropped in huge quantities to blind German radar.

The Positions

These new systems would be used to the greatest effect over Hamburg, as the city's large stretches of water showed up particularly clearly on the H2S screens of the Pathfinder aircraft leading the raids. In late July 1943, Operation Gomorrah involved Bomber Command attacking Hamburg over the course of a week, interspersed with daylight raids by the US Eighth Air Force to give the defenders no respite. To keep night fighters at bay, masses of 'Window' would produce thousands of false echoes on the early warning screens and night-fighter sets.

The Battle

The first RAF raid on the night of 24 May began just before midnight and lasted less than an hour. Almost 800 bombers found the target in clear weather with no opposition from night fighters or radar-guided anti-aircraft fire, enabling them to bomb the city centre and north-western suburbs, killing some 15 people on the ground, with only 12 bombers lost. The Americans bombed the city on the following two days and the RAF returned on the night of 26 July but high winds and thunderstorms disrupted the raid.

On the night of 27 July the RAF returned with 739 bombers, this time in ideal conditions. The bombing was much more concentrated, with large 4,000-pound (1,800 kg) 'Cookies' causing too much wreckage for fire crews to reach the area where later bombs fell. Eventually, some 600 bomb loads fell into an area measuring 3.2 by 1.6 kilometres (2 miles by 1 mile), and the superheated rising air from blazing buildings created the terrible phenomenon of a firestorm, drawing in winds strong enough to blow people into the flames and setting the tarred streets ablaze. The death toll on this single raid was estimated at 40,000 and 9.5 square kilometres (6 square miles) of the city were totally obliterated. The bombers returned in similar numbers on 29 July, but damage was reduced as the bombs fell mainly in the already burned-out areas and the recovering night fighters and AA guns brought down 28 raiders. Finally, on 3 August, bad weather gave the city a respite, while the RAF lost 30 aircraft.

The Outcome and Significance

In all, Operation Gomorrah caused the deaths of some 50,000 inhabitants of Hamburg, and more than a million people fled the city. German Armaments Minister Albert Speer estimated that six more cities destroyed on this scale would bring the nation to its knees. However, all Bomber Command's attempts to bring about a repeat of the destruction on this scale failed until the last months of the war.

Hamburg represented the most concentrated attack ever delivered on a defended German city in the area-bombing campaign, producing unprecedented destruction. It demonstrated the role aerial bombing could play, not just in hitting military and industrial targets, but also the effect of disruption and devastation on the civilian populace and morale. Its military value was less certain: post-war analyses have suggested that growing Allied bomber strength and the technology used over Hamburg could have been used to shorten the war by crippling the German oil and transport industries at an earlier stage.

Kamikaze Attacks

Where: North Pacific
When: 1944–45
War: Second World War (1939–1945)
Combatants: America vs. Japan
Casualties: Americans: 5,000; Japanese: 4,000

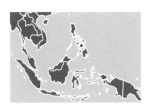

By fall 1944, the Japanese faced the largest combat fleet ever assembled, armed with more formidable aircraft and better trained crews. As the Allies forced them back to defend their homeland, they sought desperate measures to avoid inevitable defeat. During the fighting in the Philippines in October 1944, units of Japanese pilots agreed to crash their aircraft deliberately into American warships. This horrifying tactic would later grow into an organized campaign, inflicting appalling casualties on both sides. They took the name 'kamikaze' after the 'Divine Wind' typhoon that destroyed the 13th-century Mongol fleet and saved Japan from invasion.

The Positions

On 17 October, at the battle of Leyte Gulf, Japanese pilots were ordered to attack the US fleet but would face such heavy losses that their sacrifice would be pointless. Replacement pilots were too poorly trained to survive a single mission and delivering conventional attacks on heavily defended enemy warships would be impossible. Senior officers began discussing the possibility of arming Zero fighters with 500-pound (226-kg) bombs and crashing them into high-value targets. Even inexperienced pilots could find targets and accuracy would be less of a problem. Most pilots agreed enthusiastically and prepared for the first mission.

The Battle

The first suicide attack hit the Australian cruiser HMAS *Australia* on 21 October, killing 30 crew and inflicting heavy damage. Four days later, kamikazes sank the carrier USS *St. Lo* and damaged two others, with the USS

Above Gaping hole in the deck of aircraft carrier USS *Bunker Hill*, which was badly damaged after being hit twice in 30 seconds by Japanese kamikaze pilots at a cost of 656 casualties.

Intrepid being struck on 29 October. Though Japanese pilots were deeply divided – some reluctant and others enthusiastic at the results obtained – the popularity of the 'special attack units' was spreading. They hit two more carriers on the following day and had to return to base for repairs. Hits that could disable a carrier could sink smaller vessels like destroyers and the fleet had no method of dealing with this new threat, apart from spreading smoke screens across the anchorages and radioing for reinforcements. It seemed the only limit on kamikaze attacks was a shortage of planes and the difficulty of bringing pilot reinforcements into the battle area.

Kamikaze attacks reached their peak in the campaign for Okinawa in April 1945. On 6 April, 400 Japanese aircraft attacked the invasion fleet with conventional and suicide attacks. It was the kamikazes that achieved the most – six ships sunk and 18 damaged despite a furious anti-aircraft barrage and swarms of defending fighters. More attacks came on 12 and 16 April and 4 May, sinking seven ships and wrecking many more, including three battleships and three carriers. Expedients like a balloon barrage, high-altitude fighter screens and proximity-fused anti-aircraft shells helped bring down more kamikazes, but enough were getting through to inflict serious damage.

The Outcome and Significance

In all, the Japanese sent in 4,800 conventional attacks off Okinawa, with 1,465 kamikazes. Conventional bombing attacks sank one ship and damaged 63, but the far fewer suicide pilots sank seven ships and damaged 164. Later it was estimated one kamikaze in five hit a target, compared with one attack in 50 for conventional bombers, and inflicted far more resulting damage. Only the few Royal Navy carriers in the Pacific survived relatively unscathed, thanks to strongly armoured flight decks.

The Japanese suicide attacks proved lethally effective against US warships in the closing stages of the Pacific war. Kamikaze tactics were never more than a desperate short-term expedient and could never have deflected the power of the vast American fleet. However, they caused immense stress and disruption, and presented the Allies with the bleak prospect of huge casualties in their planned invasion of Japan, only avoided by the detonation of nuclear bombs on Hiroshima and Nagasaki, which brought the war to an end.

Glossary

Anzacs: Australian and New Zealand soldiers, from the initials for Australian and New Zealand Army Corps, a designation used in the First World War.

Assault gun: a tank with the turret removed and replaced with a conventional gun, to create a self-propelled, tracked and armoured artillery weapon.

Bazooka: a shoulder-mounted anti-tank rocket launcher developed in the Second World War, the ancestor of today's RPG (Rocket-Propelled Grenade) weapons.

Broadside: firing all the guns on one side of a ship's guns in a single volley, for maximum power.

Canister: a container filled with musket balls fired from cannon against enemy personnel, developed from grapeshot, which used a bag full of shot.

Carbine: a shorter version of a rifle or musket, with less power, originally used by cavalry as easier to handle on horseback.

Cartridge: a prepared charge of gunpowder that could be loaded into a gun before the shell or bullet.

Chobham armour: developed at the UK's armoured vehicle research centre at Chobham in Surrey, it uses a composite of metal and extremely hard ceramics to protect tanks from anti-tank shells.

Cookie: bombs containing high explosive within a thin casing, to blow the roofs off buildings so that incendiaries could penetrate inside and start fires.

Creeping barrage: artillery fire, where the aiming point of successive shells moves forward just ahead of advancing troops, to prevent defenders from rallying.

Discarding sabot rounds: anti-tank shells, where surrounding pieces called sabots fall away after the round leaves the barrel, leaving a smaller, tougher, high-energy dart of tungsten or depleted uranium to hit the target with maximum impact.

Drones: pilotless aircraft, controlled from the ground for reconnaissance, for bombing or simply to decoy the enemy into wasting ammunition.

Firestorm: a rapidly rising column of hot air from blazing buildings creates a partial vacuum, causing cold air to rush in and fan the flames still further, to fearsomely high temperatures.

Homing torpedo: weapon steered to its target by its noise emissions.

Katyusha: a Russian truck-mounted rocket battery firing 48 missiles at once over a range of 6.5 kilometres (4 miles), widely used by the Red Army.

Motorized infantry: support troops carried in trucks to keep up with fast-moving armoured forces.

Phalanx: a compact mass of infantry, for mutual support and shock action.

Kellermann, General François Christophe, 41
Kursk, Battle of, 1943, 92–3
Kutusov, General, 48
Kuwait, 108–9

La Haye Sainte, 50–2
Lee, General Robert E., 53–4, 55–7
Leuthen, Battle of, 1757, 37–8
longbows 26

Macedonia, 10–11
Mack, Marshal, 43
Maginot Line 78, 82, 83
Marlborough, Duke of, 34–6
Marston Moor, Battle of, 1644, 32
Massena, Marshal, 47
Meade, General George, 55–7
Midway, Battle of, 1942, 120–2
Mir Jafar, 60–1
Mir Madan, 61
Mohammed, Shah of Persia, 20–1
Mongol invasion, 1209–27, 20–1
Montgomery, Field Marshal Bernard, 89–91
Morgan, General Daniel, 39

Napoleon Bonaparte, 43–5, 46–7, 48–9, 50–2, 115
Napoleonic War, 1803–15, 43–5, 46–7, 48–9, 50–2, 114–15
Naseby, Battle of, 1645, 32–3
Nelson, Admiral Lord Horatio, 43, 114–15
Ney, Marshal, 43, 50
Norman Conquest, 1066, 18–19
Normandy, Battle of, 1944, 99–101
North African Campaign, 1941, 85–6, 89–91

Okinawa, Battle of, 1945, 139
Operation Desert Storm, 1991, 108–9
Operation Gomorrah, 1943, 135–6

Patton, General George, 84, 100
Paulus, Field Marshal von, 96
Pearl Harbor, 1941, 118–19, 120
Percival, Lieutenant General Arthur, 88
Persian Empire, 10–11, 20–21
Philip II, king of Spain, 112
Philip, king of France, 25
Pickett, General George E., 55–7
Plassey, Battle of, 1757, 60–1
Prussia, 37–8, 41–2, 50–2
Pulleine, Colonel, 66

radar, 132–4, 135
Raevsky redoubt, 49
riflemen, 39–40
Robert the Bruce, 22–4
Roman Empire, 12–13, 14–15, 16–17
Rommel, Field Marshall Erwin, 86, 89–91
Rorke's Drift, Battle of, 1879, 68–9
Rupert, Prince, 32
Russia, 43–5, 48–9, 72–3, 92–3, 94–6, 116–17
Russo–Japanese War, 1904–5, 116–17

Saddam Hussein, 108
schiltrons, 22–4
Scotland, 22–4
Second Punic War, 218–210 BCE, 12–13
Second World War, 1939–45, 82–4, 85–6, 87–8, 89–91, 92–3, 94–6, 97–8, 99–101, 118–19, 120–2, 123–5, 132–4, 135–6, 137–9
Senlac Hill, 18–19
Seven Years' War, 1756–63, 37–8, 60–1
Singapore, Battle of, 1942, 87–8
Siraj-ud-Daulah, Nawab of Bengal, 60–1
Somme, Battle of the, 1916, 76–8
Soult, Marshal, 44
Spain, 112–13, 114–15
Spanish Invasion Campaign, 1588, 112–13

Stalingrad, Battle of, 1942–3, 94–6
Stanford Bridge, Battle of, 1066, 18–19
Stuart, Jeb, 54
Sweden, 30–1

Tallard, Marshall, 34–6
tanks, 79–81, 84
Tannenberg, Battle of, 1914, 72–3
Tarawa, Battle of, 1943, 97–8
Tarleton, Lieutenant Colonel Banastre, 39–40
Tet offensive, 107
Teutoburg Forest, Battle of the, 9 CE, 16–17
Thirty Years' War, 1618–48, 30–1
Tilly, Count of, 30
Togo, Admiral, 116
Torres Vedras, Battle of, 1810–11, 46–7
Trafalgar, Battle of, 1805, 43, 114–15
Tsushima, Battle of, 1905, 116–17
Turkey, 74–5

U-boats, 123–5
United States, 39–40, 53–4, 55–7, 97–8, 106–7, 118–19, 120–2, 137–9

Valmy, Battle of, 1792, 41–2
Vercingetorix, 14–15
Verdun, Battle of, 1916, 76–8
Versailles, Treaty of, 1918, 82
Vicksburg, siege of, 55–7
Vietnam War, 1959–75, 106–7
Vietnam, 104–5, 106–7
Villeneuve, Admiral, 114

Wallace, William, 22
War of the Spanish Succession, 1701–14, 34–6
Waterloo, Battle of, 1815, 50–2
Wellington, Duke of, 46–7, 50–2
William, Duke of Normandy, 18–19

Zeppelin raids, 1915, 130–1
Zulu War, 1879, 65–7, 68–9

This edition first published in 2009 by
New Holland Publishers (UK) Ltd
London • Cape Town • Sydney • Auckland
www.newhollandpublishers.com

Garfield House, 86–88 Edgware Road, London
W2 2EA, United Kingdom

2 4 6 8 10 9 7 5 3 1

Conceived and produced by
Elwin Street Productions
144 Liverpool Road
London N1 1LA
www.elwinstreet.com

ISBN-13: 978-1-84773-644-4

Cover Design: Vanessa Green, The Urban Ant Ltd
Design and icon illustration: James Lawrence
All other illustrations: Richard Burgess

Picture credits:
Alamy: pp. 16, 63, 90, 95; Corbis: pp. 77;
Getty: pp. 35, 105, 119, 124, 137;
Imperial War Museum: p. 87.

Printed and bound in China

David Owen has written more than 20 books ranging
from military history to forensic science, and from
espionage to criminal profiling. He is the author of
The Little Book of Forensics and *Espionage*.